# SpringerBriefs in Business



For further volumes:
http://www.springer.com/series/8860

Jiazhuo G. Wang · Juan Yang

# Who Gets Funds from China's Capital Market?

## A Micro View of China's Economy via Case Studies on Listed Chinese SMEs

Springer

Jiazhuo G. Wang
School of Business
College of Staten Island
City University of New York
New York, NY
USA

Juan Yang
HSBC Business School
Peking University
Shenzhen, Guangdong
People's Republic of China

ISSN 2191-5482 ISSN 2191-5490 (electronic)
ISBN 978-3-642-44912-3 ISBN 978-3-642-44913-0 (eBook)
DOI 10.1007/978-3-642-44913-0
Springer Heidelberg New York Dordrecht London

Library of Congress Control Number: 2013957358



Printed on acid-free paper

Springer is part of Springer Science+Business Media (www.springer.com)

# Preface

Why China? About 20 years ago, when China's Shanghai Stock Exchange and Shenzhen Stock Exchange were re-opened and newly established in 1990, this would have been the typical question that foreign investors would ask had they been suggested to take a look at these just-born capital markets. Even about 14 years later, when the Shenzhen Stock Exchange introduced its small and medium enterprises board (SME Board) in May of 2004, many continued to hold a skeptical view of the Chinese capital markets, believing it to still be in its infancy.

It was true that, if those skeptics were right, then indeed, why China? From a foreign investor's perspective, China's stock market was still way too "green" in many aspects, especially compared with its counterparts in New York, London, Frankfort, Tokyo, Singapore, or even Hong Kong which, after its time under the British Commonwealth in twentieth century, was returned to China's jurisdiction in 1997. Among the many shortcomings of China's growing capital market, incomplete and insufficient regulations, ineffective law enforcement, unreliable accounting information and disclosure, and unsustainable business models that were unable to generate sustainable future cash flows deterred the interests of the potential investors from China's capital market.

Even to this day, the improvement of law enforcement and the quality of financial information and disclosure may still appear as an ever-present issue. However, significant progress has undoubtedly been observed on the regulation side, and in the innovation of business models in China in the past two decades. In particular, these business models, developed by companies across all kinds of industries, have fundamentally changed the way that people used to think, look at and evaluate Chinese companies.

There are a number of possible reasons for why these new business models have begun to be developed in the past few decades.

Come to the first is the most straightforward one, which is the volatile economic climate of the last decade and the increased competition in the market place that have inevitably encouraged innovation-driven companies. Not too long ago, as the "workshop of the world," China was feeding the whole world with almost everything people need in their daily life. This was made possible by the support of China's abundant labor forces released continuously from China's rural areas and the no-one-can-beat-it prices on the global market. Taking advantage of its entry into WTO and the overwhelming demand from the world (especially those from the major developed markets), China was able to reclaim a period of the "shortage era," when demand was not an issue and producing whatever the world needed at the most competitive pricing was the only game to be played. In those good old days, any business model other than "lowest possible pricing" seemed obsolete.

But every party has its end, and it is true for both China and the world. The highly leveraged consumption model that had helped create the longest expansion period in the USA history since World War II eventually triggered a worldwide financial crisis and the deepest recession since the Great Depression of the 1920s. Meanwhile, China's export-investment oriented, low-cost labor driven growth model also seemed to come as close as it possibly could to an end. When the first wave of the economic tsunami flooded in, unsurprisingly, it was the companies that had survived for so long on the thread of tiny price margins and a "make a quick buck" philosophy that were the first to get blown aside. At the same time, the companies that were built up on stronger values and unique business models unambiguously stood their ground. Only these companies, those with long-term visions, a focus on long-run brand buildup and strategic business model development became the companies that eventually picked the cherry on the top of the tree.

The second and potentially more pressing reason for business model innovation may have stemmed from Chinese companies need to get financing, which, intrinsically, requires more depth of discussion. As many may know, financing for small and medium sized enterprises (SME) is always a challenging issue, not only in China, but also globally. The difficulties in getting financing for SMEs may result from a number of SMEs' inherent characteristics, and also of the risks inherited by financing smaller businesses. Just to name a few, these characteristics and risks may include:

(a) Asymmetric information. The outsiders of a company always know less than the insiders about what actually goes on at a firm. It is not only true for publicly traded large corporations, but also, and especially for SMEs. Either due to cost considerations or protection concerns, SMEs typically disclose less information to the general public than their larger corporate counterparts. As a result, SMEs are typically perceived as enterprises with much higher degrees of uncertainty and risk.
(b) Non-standardized financial information. In addition to less information released to the general public, the financial information possessed by the SMEs is also less likely to be standardized in a format that is in compliance with the generally accepted accounting principles. Due to limited resources, SMEs usually cannot afford to hire financial professionals to prepare their financial documents, or contract public accounting firms to audit their financial statements. As a consequence, even when SMEs consent to providing their documents, not much of the information can be actually used by financial institutions when they make financing decisions toward SMEs.
(c) Lack of adequate collateral for bank loans. Because these firms are small, the amount of assets that they can use as collateral for bank loans are typically less. When compared against the financing values that most SMEs request and

need, the collateral they possessed are usually not adequate to meet the requirements of banks.

(d) Insufficiency of credit records. Commercial banks typically need to use the credit history of their borrowers as an important reference when making financing decisions. However, many SMEs usually don't have any history of borrowing money from banks due to the difficulties in securing bank loans as described above. As a consequence, they are usually rejected for bank loans due to the lack of credit history. Clearly, this creates a vicious cycle. If a SME doesn't have adequate credit history, it won't be able to get credit; if it cannot get credit, it is almost cyclically banned from ever being able to obtain a loan.

(e) Management flexibility in changing a firm's risk. The classical agency problem normally occurs in large corporations due to the separation of ownership and management. Small businesses usually can avoid this problem because the owner and manager are typically the same person. However, retaining the functionality of ownership and management in one person may increase the flexibility, in both a positive and a negative sense, of the firm's operations. On the one hand, small businesses can change the direction of their businesses or the composition of the firm's assets more easily and rapidly in response to the changes in technology or business conditions. At the same time, however, this flexibility may also increase the uncertainty about the future operations and development of the firm, hence, increasing the firm's risk.

(f) Lack of economy of scale as a disincentive for financial institutions. From the perspective of the commercial banks, no matter the size of the firm that requests the loans, the bank must input the same amount of effort and procedure to clear that firm for lending; that is, the same application reviews, credit assessment, comprehensive analysis, on-site investigation, and final release of funds, all of which are heavy uses of time and resources. Given the relatively smaller size of loans to SMEs comparing with ones to larger corporations, it is difficult for the commercial banks to achieve the same economy of scale when lending to SMEs. Needless to say, commercial banks, on the whole, prefer larger corporations.

For SMEs, this financing issue is even more severe in China as its economy is still in a transition from a centrally planned regime to a completely market-oriented one. So in addition to the issues that are shared in common with SMEs in developed countries, SMEs in China face the additional burden of even more limited numbers of financial institutions that can legally provide funding to them, which in turn exacerbates the imbalance between demand and supply in the loanable funds market in China. For many years since its inception, the financial industry in China has been so highly regulated that only large, state-owned commercial banks were allowed to be major fund suppliers. Private funds were typically not permitted to directly enter the market. From an economic perspective, under this regime, providing their already limited funds to larger, state-owned (nonfinancial) corporations was clearly a better choice for the large, state-owned commercial banks, considering all the risks and possible returns. As a consequence, many illegal "shadow loans" with annualized interest rates as high as up to 50 % emerged in some of the more developed areas in China in the recent years,[1] in an attempt to fill the gap in funding supply. And it's no surprise that these "illegal" financing activities generated tremendous risks and had the potential to trigger financial crises in various forms.

Considering this background, the development of Chinese public equity markets in the past few decades (as benchmarked by the opening of the Shanghai and Shenzhen Stock Exchanges) did in fact provide an important new funding source for SMEs in China. The happy news was that, since 2004, when the SME Board of Shenzhen Stock Exchange established, an increasing number of SME stocks have been listed in both the Shenzhen Stock Exchange's SME Board and that of the Second Board (Growth Enterprise Board), which was established in 2009. By June 2013, 701 and 355 SME stocks have been listed in these two boards, growing 88 and 13 times, respectively, compared with the numbers from 2004. The total market value also increased from 41.3 billion RMB to about 4.4 trillion RMB during the same period of time, increasing by about 109 times.[2]

The hard part was that in order to get funds from equity investors, the SMEs that were looking for equity capital must meet the expectations of the equity investors. Because they are making a long-term investment, equity investors focus not only on the historical performance of a firm, they also look at the future cash flows that, together with the inherited risks associated with the companies' earnings, determines the value of the firm; only a sustainable future cash flow would maximize the wealth of equity shareholders. The question, then, was on what parameters should equity investors judge the future cash flows of these SMEs?

As the age of low cost and low pricing gives way to a different kind of competitive market, generating a sustainable cash flow, on the business side, is now anchored upon well-designed business models and flawless execution. A well-designed business model needs to adequately address all the strategic issues facing the firm for its long-term development, which include, but are not limited to, which industry the firm should be in? What products/services they should produce? What kind of relationships does the firm need to build with its customers, suppliers, and venders so as to minimize cost or increase profit? And most importantly, what unique business model does the firm need to create to distinguish itself from its closest competitor(s), and how can they highlight their core competencies? In the post-financial crisis era, a well-designed and well executed business model will become the ace that distinguishes the winners from the losers, not only in the goods/services market but in the financial market as well.

In the last 20 years, the question of "why China" has been near completely muted as China's capital markets gradually improve in value, and the opportunities

---

1 Wall Street Journal: http://online.wsj.com/article/SB1000142405297020391430457662694181 3821726.html

2 Shenzhen Stock Exchange: http://www.szse.cn/main/marketdata/, Sohu Security: http://stock.sohu.com/20091225/n269197316.shtml

that Chinese companies can offer have been increasingly revealed on a global scale. During the past 20 years, Chinese capital markets have been re-categorized by many portfolio managers worldwide from a "transitional investment" to a "permanent allocation." Many top-notch investors such as Warren Buffet, George Soros, and Jim Rogers, and many active private equity funds and investment banking houses such as Bain Capital, Blackstone, Goldman Sachs, and Morgan Stanley, have appeared on the list of Chinese equity investors. It is the Chinese companies with solid, unique business models, among other distinguishing characteristics, that have been hungrily chased by investors both inside and outside China.

Like in the USA, SMEs comprises over 99 % of the total number of Chinese companies.[3] The 1,000 or so companies listed in the SME Board and Second Board only represent a very small fraction of the total Chinese companies that need external financing. Without a question, these SMEs that were listed on China's capital market are among the most elite ones. Who are these "lucky guys" that received funds from China's competitive capital market, and what did they bring to the table that caused them to be China's financial markets' favored stars? Answers to these questions are certainly among some of the most intriguing and sought out to both Chinese and foreign readerships.

The general interest in this issue of China's SMEs and the capital markets is a result of the huge role that China is expected to play in world economic growth in the forthcoming decades. It is also a result of the highly interconnected and interdependent global market that is now an economic reality. Although the Chinese economy revealed signs for slowdown in the past quarters, its role as one of the most powerful engines for worldwide economic growth in the next decades is still indisputable. Even more unavoidable is China's ever-growing purchasing power that has been accumulating over the past 30 years by an over 9 % average annual growth rate, and its production and export capacity as "the workshop of the world". Most importantly, its ambitious urbanization plan from about 50 % as of current to about 75 % in the next 30 years[4] will alone generate another market the size of the currently existing China market.

As one of the major sources fueling China's enormous growth engine, the Chinese financial markets and their activity—which cover over 99 % of all Chinese companies—is both a critical and extremely fascinating issue for anyone who may be interested in or impacted by the Chinese market in the coming years.

In particular, institutional and individual investors both inside and outside China should be finding this topic relevant and intriguing. Financial institutions such as security firms, investment banks, private equity funds, venture capitals, commercial banks, other financial intermediaries, and individual investors

[3] Zibin Li, President of Chinese SME Association, Xinhua News Net: http://news.xinhuanet.com/fortune/2010-05

[4] Wall Street Journal: http://online.wsj.com/article/SB10001424052970203735304577166652002366514.html

including angels could all do well with watching China's financial market closely. Given the interconnected nature of the global financial markets and the complementary nature of different segments/areas of the financial markets, what kinds of Chinese SMEs that can eventually be listed and traded publicly, what stories were brought by the SMEs to convince the market, and what kind of returns for Pre-IPO investors obtained at the exit will be undoubtedly relevant to all these investors, and in turn, will also influence investors' investment decisions at all stages of the target companies' financial growth cycle.

The Chinese SMEs that are looking for public equity funding should also take interest in this topic. The products, the industries, the business models, and the growth potential these listed SMEs promised are solid indicators for what investors prefer and where they are willing to put their money.

Foreign companies, especially foreign SMEs that are looking for external funding from overseas market, are impacted as well. Given the abundant funds available in China's current market and an increased possibility of an opening of an international board in China to list foreign companies, understanding what kinds of Chinese SMEs are already listed would certainly be instructional for them.

Finally, the academia inside and outside China should also take interest, for a number of reasons:

(a) China's sustainable economic growth in the next decades truly depends upon whether or not China can successfully transfer its growth model from the past 30 years to a new one in the next 30 years, that is, transferring from an investment and export driven way to a domestic consumption driven one, from an environment-damaging, energy-wasting method to an environmentally-friendly and energy-saving one, and, finally, transferring from competing on low labor cost to competing on branding and technology innovation.
(b) More and more people realize that technology innovation is not a pure "technology" concept, as Joseph Schumpeter indicated decades ago.[5] Instead, tech innovation is an economic concept that involves in an entire process of research, development, production, marketing, consumption and feedback about an innovation of a product, a service or a business model. As a result, entrepreneurs, instead of scientists and engineers, are the primary participants of the innovation process.
(c) Since over 99 % of Chinese companies are SMEs, active participation of SMEs will undoubtedly determine the success of technology innovation and the transformation of China's future growth models.
(d) Given the economic nature of tech innovation, receiving adequate financing will be a determining factor of new innovation development, especially for the tech innovation initiated by SMEs. Consequently, understanding what kinds of SMEs can obtain funds from China's public equity market and how they got

[5] Schumpeter, J., 2006, Capitalism, Socialism and Democracy, New Edition, Routledge, London.

the funding is certainly of significant value in research on the sustainability of China's future growth and design of China's continued reform for the next 30 years.

(e) Needless to say, China is one of the most powerful engines for today's global economic growth. As a result, the sustainability of global economic growth is highly correlated with the sustainability of China's growth in the forthcoming decades. As many studies about China's business and economy so far only focused on the macro side of the Chinese economy and these aggregate numbers such as the level and growth rate of GDP, inflation, unemployment rate, interest rate, and exchange rate, research on the Chinese economy from micro view and at the level of company, the basic unit of any economy, to analyze the key industries, representative companies, and successful business models that the Chinese firms developed and adopted in operating in today's market place will be an important complement for the knowledge and understanding about Chinese economy.

Therefore, we think this concise book could be a timely publication with significant value for a wide spectrum of readerships either as a reference book or as a guideline in understanding, in gaining knowledge, in research and teaching, and in making business decisions about China and about many other global issues with China connectivity.

# Acknowledgments

This book is the joint effort of a research team consisting of faculty and graduate students from the City University of New York, the Small and Medium Enterprises Research Center, and the HSBC School of Business at Peking University.

Between the authors, Dr. Jiazhuo G. Wang wrote the Preface and the last chapter, Chap. 11. Dr. Juan Yang wrote Chap. 1, the Introduction to China's SME and GEM markets. Kai Zhu selected the nine cases from the compilation of Chinese companies listed on the SME and GEM boards of China's stock market, and drafted the Chinese version of the case in Chap. 10. Yang Ge drafted the Chinese version of the cases in Chaps. 4, 8 and 9. Tangren Feng drafted the Chinese version of the cases in Chaps. 5–7. Jie Zou drafted the Chinese version of the cases in Chaps. 2 and 3. Yalan Liu provided the initial English translation for the cases in Chaps. 2, 4, 9 and 10. Yue Zhang provided the initial English translation for the cases in Chaps. 5–7. Yuping Yun provided initial English translation for the cases in Chaps. 3 and 8. Drs. Jiazhuo G. Wang and Juan Yang reviewed and revised all chapters and finalized the book for its submission.

In addition, Allison Wang of the Stern School of Business at New York University edited and proofread the entire book, which greatly enhanced its readability. The editor of Springer Publisher, Toby Chai, initiated the book writing on Chinese business and economy, and provided much support along with the production of this book. All the efforts and contributions of the above individuals toward the publication of this book are greatly appreciated. Of course, the authors are solely responsible for any errors and omissions.

# Contents

# Chapter 1
# SME and SME Board of China's Capital Market

**Abstract** As all the cases studied in this book focus on small and medium enterprises (SME), specifically those that were listed on the SME board of China's Shenzhen Stock Exchange, this chapter provides the readers with an overview about SMEs in China and development of the SME board that hosted listing the companies cased in this book.

**Keywords** SME · SME board · Equity financing · State-owned firms · Privately-owned enterprises

As the cases of the selected SMEs that were listed in China's capital market will be presented and discussed one by one in the following chapters, it may be beneficial for the readers to first take an overview about small and medium sized enterprises (SME) and the SME board of stock exchange in China that hosts the companies that will be discussed in this book. It is the background of the cases or stories that are contained in this book.

## 1.1 A Turbulent Time for SMEs in China

When talking about small and medium-sized enterprises (SMEs) in China, several statistics, typically, will likely be referred to the status-de-qua of SMEs. In China, SMEs account for over 99 % of the total number of firms, over 60 % of China's GDP, over 50 % of total tax revenue, and over 80 % of total employment.[1] It is no question that SMEs' development has significant impacts on China's overall economy.

Since 2011, however, bad news has come in a throng on SMEs in China. Many garment factories in Guangzhou, a major exporting city in southern China, shut down due to a sharp drop in orders from overseas. Jiangnan Leather, Portman, and

[1] Zibin Li, President of Chinese SME Association, Xinhua News: http://news.xinhuanet.com/fortune/2010-05

J. G. Wang and J. Yang, *Who Gets Funds from China's Capital Market?*,
SpringerBriefs in Business, DOI: 10.1007/978-3-642-44913-0_1, 

Sanqi Group, three well-known SMEs in Wenzhou, one of SMEs' most developed areas in China, all came on the verge of bankruptcy as their owners fled away due to the cut down of their fund chain. Even by the end of 2008, lots of SMEs were already forced to close their shops as impacted by financial crisis. After nearly 3 years of recovery, when China's general economic condition has been observed to start bottom up, the SMEs, in contrary to the expectations by many, seem still to be in a situation "even harder than in 2008".

Why did that happen? There were a number of issues that can be identified over there: the rising cost in labor and raw materials, the appreciation of RMB, and the shortage of labor, energy and capital in the post financial crisis time, to just name a few, all imposed pronounced threat on SMEs survival and success. Mr. Zhou, Dewen, the President of Small and Medium Enterprise Association of Wenzhou City, a city located in southeastern Zhejiang Province and famous for being a birthplace of China's private enterprises and cradle of SMEs, spoke to news reporters recently that "if the existing tightened monetary policy doesn't change and government doesn't step in, 40 % of existing small and medium sized businesses will go out of business within a half year."[2] In fact, what Mr. Zhou warned about for Wenzhou SMEs actually happened almost everywhere in China including both Pearl River Delta and Yangzi River Delta, the China's two most developed areas.

It, then, may seem strange on the first glance why the SMEs in China are still like infants that never grow up even after so many years' development, and cause the curiosity for what may be the root causes underlying the phenomenon.

The concept of SMEs in China is far more complicated than its literal meaning, and it also goes beyond the notions of the typical official definitions in terms of size of personnel, assets and the scope of the business operations. It is an ever-changing concept, and its change largely reflects the transition of China's political and economic structure, which, to some degree, plays a vital role in the survival and success of SMEs in China.

As an ambitious plan to change the country, China's reform and opening up to outside world starting in late 1970s were actually originated from an anxiety that "productivity" that were generated by Chinese economy was unable to back up China's institutional legitimacy that was expected. It also coincided with the desire of the average citizens of the country then that lived with only extremely scarce material resources to eradicate poverty. Therefore, staring from the rural areas in the late 1970s, extended to the urban areas in the mid-1980s, the enthusiasm of the long repressed civil society for creating wealth was greatly released.

During this period of time, SMEs had come into play energetically taking the forms of Township-and-Village-Owned Enterprises and Collectively-Owned enterprises. Meanwhile, there were two strong external forces that stimulated the developments of SMEs. The first one was the huge domestic demand for basic consumption goods, and the second was the strong support from local

2 "Who will save the SMEs?", *South Reviews*, Vol. 13, 2011.

governments. After 1994, the SMEs in China gradually transformed and converged to only two categories: state-owned firms and privately-owned enterprises. Meanwhile, the external environment for conducting business also changed tremendously. Compared to the 1980s, the export had become the dominant driving engine of China's economy, and GDP had been considered the major evaluation metric on the local government performance. To those private enterprises, these changes provided even better business opportunities. SMEs continued receiving the large amount of support in terms of funds, lands and tax deductions from various government agencies.

The situations changed since 2005, however, and since then China's new ownership structure has been established. The government policies that only focus on invigorating large scaled state-owned enterprises and leave the smaller ones to market for their fates made the SMEs basically being the synonym of private owned enterprises. Such new structure endowed the state-owned enterprises with giant market share and institutional privilege while repressed the SMEs to the other end which were barely entitled any favorable public assistance. The significant need for financial support and very limited financing channels available for SMEs has become the bottle neck of SME's development in China.

Since then, SMEs underwent tremendous hardships in the recent years and only very few SMEs have successfully not only survived but also grown well through such a disturbance age. As a reality, more SMEs currently still have their backs to the wall.

Of course, while each company may have different issues in technical, operational or management areas, the common and urgent one is how to get the funding to finance their businesses. Therefore, the SMEs that succeeded in obtaining funding are of great value for millions of its peers. This book selects 9 representative cases from China's SMEs in various industries, which have pulled off a successful public offering in China's capital market, and their stories may give more SMEs that were still in struggle some insights in their future development.

## 1.2 The Challenges for Financing SMEs

Many SMEs complain that it is difficult to get financed in China. But that doesn't mean it is impossible. If it is truly impossible to get financed in China at all for SMEs, why has the BYD,[3] a SME car maker, grown so fast? Why did Wang, Chuanfu, the CEO of BYD, top Forbes China Rich list? One of the possible answers is that BYD played the "trick" of finance well. A successful company should not only know how to manage its internal financial sources, but also need to

[3] BYD Co Ltd is a Chinese manufacturer of automobiles and rechargeable batteries based in Shenzhen, Guangdong Province. BYD topped the 2010 Bloomberg Business week Tech 100 list, a list of large, fast growth tech companies. The founder and chairman of BYD is Wang Chuanfu.

know how to fully utilize the external financing as well. Not only handle well physical asset, but also its financial assets. One can imagine that if a company only relies on its own resources, it may never be able to really grow big, only if does it know how to make good use of outside resources including financial resources.

Having said this, however, it is still true that, in China, SMEs are still confronted with great difficulties in getting financed due to the reasons that have been mentioned in the preface of this book, such as poor credit history, insufficient collaterals, the unfavorable financing policies of financial institutions, and lack of support from government regulations, to just name a few. As is well known, in general, there are two major external funding sources for a company. One is the direct financing channel in which funds were obtained by firm directly from the fund providers through financial market by selling securities such as stocks or bonds. The other one is the indirect financing channel where a financial intermediary such as commercial banks first takes the money from a lender (such as depositors), then lend to a borrower (either consumers or companies). Unfortunately, both channels are quite limited to SMEs to raise the funds in China now.

A research from the World Bank[4] shows that the development funds for China's private-owned company mostly came from owner's own capital and its company's retaining earnings. The percentage of the funding through bond and equity issuance is quite small, and, as mentioned earlier, SMEs in China have reached a severe bottleneck of direct financing.

As experienced in both developed and developing countries, equity financing could greatly help SMEs get the long-term stable funding and improve the firms' capital structure. Taking a Chinese company as an example, Vanke Real Estate, the largest residential real estate developer in China and headquartered in Shenzhen, Guangdong Province, made its IPO in 1988 and raised the fund of RMB 28 million. Since then it accumulatively collected the total amount of RMB 5.1 billion through 6 rounds of refinancing, and completed a magnificent transformation from a small and unknown company to a real estate giant in China.[5] During such a transition, the long term and stable capital that Vanke secured from stock market made an indelible contribution.

Different from debt financing through borrowing from banks, the equity financing does not impose the pressure on company for paying back the principal and interest, and mitigates the risk of bankruptcy. Therefore company can devote more funds to R&D and other longer run projects that may not be able to generate cash inflows in the short period of time, and it will benefit the company in the long run and effectively enhance the company's incentive and capability for continued innovation.

---

[4] World Bank International Finance Corporation, "China's Emerging Private Enterprises: Prospects For The New Century", p. 50, also available at: http://www.ifc.org/wps/wcm/connect/publications_ext_content/ifc_external_publication_site/

[5] International Association of Entrepreneurs: http://www.hk-assoc.org/en/?action-viewnews-itemid-520

It may be true that, going public, get into money heaven; if not, fall into hell. Thanks to the most recently released information by China Security Regulatory Commission (CSRC), China's SEC, we learned how tough for SMEs to be listed in China's capital market. The CSRC report released in June 2012 showed that there were 380 companies that had submitted application documents to CSRC for IPO by then, during which 139 companies were under first round review, 124 were about to receive the review feedback, 54 completed information disclosure, 58 were approved, and 10 companies stopped application. The total application number rose to 758 in September 2012. From the first quarter of 2011 to the third quarter of 2012, the approval rate of SME board, 72.3 %, is the lowest compared to 90 % of main board, and 81.9 % of GEM Board.[6] Considering the case of failure in the preview stage or suspension which is not counted in the approval rate, the success rate would be even lower.

The ancient Greece mathematician Archimedes once stated that "Give me a place to stand and with a lever I will move the whole world."[7] For SMEs, go public is such a spot to stand. Some good SMEs with great potentials can grow rapidly into an industry giant with the help of the capital market to raise the needed funds. Therefore, going public of course becomes the chasing goal of many SMEs, and the SME board of China's capital market is naturally the most popular choice for its customized feature when hosting the SMEs.

## 1.3 The SME Board: A Cradle for Invisible SME Champions

The development of China's public equity market in the recent years, particularly the establishment of SME board, provided new funding sources for SMEs in China. Since the establishment of SME Board of Shenzhen Stock Exchange in 2004, an increasing number of SME stocks have been listed in the SME Board, and a number of famous companies also grew up from this board. No wonder that the SME board is widely considered the cradle of SME champions. Up to May 2012, over 600 stocks have been listed in this board, increasing by over 80 times comparing with the numbers in 2004. The total market value also increased to about 4 trillion RMB during the same period of time, increasing by almost 100 times.

In fact, the establishment of SME board not only fostered the popular stars among SMEs, more importantly, it channeled the funds to the fastest growing companies with most potentials. Those star companies were live demonstrations of the miracles achieved through the capital market, and attracted many venture capitals starting to focus on SMEs thereafter. Massive SMEs therefore obtained

6 http://stock.jrj.com.cn/focus/20120608,zhuban/

7 http://www.math.nyu.edu/~crorres/Archimedes/Lever/LeverQuotes.html

more funds from capital market, and the listing in the SME board became the goal for many well run companies. Thus these public-company-hopefuls provided the continuous supply of candidates for listing in SME boards.

Meanwhile, the establishment and development of SME boards means a lot to investors. In the past 8 years since the launch of SME board, every investor who concerned about SME board has been pain and happy in turns. As an important layer of multi-level capital market, whether the SME board could be the catalyst for rapid growth of numerous SMEs has been the topic of most concern. The good sign is that only less than 1 % of 672 listed companies in SME board had been "specially treated"[8] because of their poor performance. 99 % of listed companies in SME board have survived in the last round of global financial crisis and displayed the strong vitality, indicating that the management of SME board is quite strict and did decent due diligence when scrutinizing and approving the companies to be listed.

The good qualifications of listed companies in SME board make it the favorite investment choice for many investors in China. For example, in July 2004, Suning Appliance Company, one of the largest privately owned electrical appliance retailers in China, listed on the SME board in the Shenzhen Stock Exchange, opened at RMB 29.88 per share and rallied to RMB 71.48 in just 8 months, and became the first high-priced shares in Shanghai and Shenzhen Stock Exchange.[9] Moreover, Suning pays dividends every year and has maintained the cash cow status in the stock market since then. In addition to Suning, Huayi Brother, BYD, Eternal Asia and many more superior companies also grew into industry giants with the help of the capital market.[10] While they became the stars by getting funds from SME board, they also provided great investment opportunities to vast investors.

Therefore, what is the secret for these companies to be successfully listed in the SME board? What stories did these companies bring to the capital market to help them get funds? The following chapters of this book will reveal some unique strategies and business models behind those successfully listed SMEs in China for the first time.

---

[8] The companies with poor business performance will be marked as ST (Specially Treated) companies in the stock market and it warns the investors of the risk of delisting for these companies.

[9] WIND Financial Market Database in China.

[10] The detailed cases about these companies will be discussed in the subsequent chapters.

# Chapter 2
# The Power of Batteries: The Story of BYD

**Abstract** This chapter discusses the case of BYD, a leading new-energy powered carmaker in China. Its vision capitalizes on the trend of emerging new energy industries, and the case will examine its ability to integrate business lines to generate synergies and its unique business development model that has attracted global investors including Warren Buffet.

**Keywords** New energy · Rechargeable batteries · New-energy-powered automobiles · Electric-power storage stations · Vertical integration · Industry chain

On September 29, 2008, Warrant Buffett announced his USD $230 million investment to acquire 10 % of shares of a Chinese company called BYD, a firm that makes the next-generation batteries, electric cars and consumer electronics parts. BYD was actually the second Chinese company that Warren Buffett chose to invest. Since then, the price of BYD stock shoot to the roof, jumping nearly 10 times, and the initial investment of Buffet also appreciated from $230 million to $2.3 billion in merely one year. As an investor famous on gains from long-holding strategies, the speed and rate of return for his investment in BYD may seem a sweat "surprise" for Warren Buffet. No question, the "secret" for BYD's success for both its business and its getting such a favor from Warren Buffett and the global financial market would be intriguing, and let's take a close look at it.

## 2.1 A Fast Growing Legend

BYD, founded in 1995 by Chuangfu Wang, is a privately-owned, high-tech company. It started as a firm producing rechargeable batteries, but later expanded its business territory to new-energy-powered automobiles and new energy industries, and gained market dominance in a fast pace. BYD is widely recognized as the leader in the rechargeable battery industry, and meanwhile, a rising star in the markets of electric automobiles, electric-power storage systems, and solar power stations. BYD was listed on Hong Kong Stock Exchange (Ticker: 0285.HK) in

J. G. Wang and J. Yang, *Who Gets Funds from China's Capital Market?*,
SpringerBriefs in Business, DOI: 10.1007/978-3-642-44913-0_2, 

2007 and in Shenzhen Stock Exchange (Ticker: 002594) in 2011, respectively. In total, BYD has 2.354 billion outstanding shares, and 33.69 % of which, or 793 million, are H shares. The founder Chuangfu Wang, as the single largest shareholder of the firm, owning 570 million shares, which account for about 24.24 % of the firm's total capitalization.[1] In 2010, BYD was ranked the first place among the Top-100 IT companies, and the number 8th among the Top-50 The Most Creative Companies in the world (ranked the number one in China) by the Business Week.

The rechargeable battery products of BYD can actually be further decomposed into lithium battery, MH-Ni battery, as well as solar cell and components. As the leading company in the rechargeable battery industry, BYD mainly serves these primary phone producers such as Nokia, Samsung, MOTO (Motorola), Huawei, ZTE, and electric tool and portable electronics producers such as Bosch and TTI. According to a report released by the Institute of Information Technology (IIT), the lithium battery market share captured by Japan, a major lithium battery producer in the world has been shrinking in the recent years. At the same time, however, the market share of the lithium battery produced by BYD has been increasing, about 6.6 % in 2009, and 8.75 % in 2010. Meanwhile, BYD is the largest producer of the MH-Ni battery in the world where its competitors in this market include Sanyo, Panasonic and MBI.[2] As for the solar cell and components lines of BYD, it also increased dramatically in the past years. BYD's total sales revenue reached RMB 5.004 billion in 2010 with an annual increase of 18.28 %, largely due to the fast growth of its solar cell and components, which already accounted for 15.16 % of BYD's total sales revenue.

At the same time, BYD has been continuously making efforts in the new-energy-powered automobiles, electric-power storage stations and PV power stations by utilizing its leading-edge battery technologies. In 2003, BYD acquired the Xi'an Qinchuan Auto Co., Ltd. (now BYD Auto Co., Ltd.) to start entering into the auto making industry. Since then, BYD's compounding growth rate for the auto making business has reached 74.88 % during the 2008–2010 time span, and now it is ranked the sixth largest auto maker in China by the China Association of Automobile Manufacturers, and the largest among the domestic-non-joint-venture car producers.[3] On the financial side, BYD's car business achieved revenue of RMB 48.82 billion, net profit of 1.385 billion, and EPS 0.6 Yuan in 2011. From 2007 to 2011, the average annual growth rate of BYD's car business revenue reached about 20.76 %, and the net profit 10.68 %. In 2011 alone, BYD sold 1,222 new-energy-powered cars with an increase of 480 cars over 2010. BYD's auto business now becomes the major source of its total sales revenue, accounting for about 50 % of the BYD's total sale revenue.

---

[1] All data for BYD are from Prospectus of BYD, 2011 unless indicated otherwise.

[2] *Worldwide Market Update on NiMH, Li Ion and Polymer Batteries for Portable and the Future Applications*, Institute of Information Technology (IIT), 2010.

[3] Analyst Report on BYD, Guotai Junan Securities, 2011.

So the question is, what actually happened behind these magical numbers, and what business models and strategies powered BYD for its fast development and drove BYD to where it is today. Let's take a closer look.

## 2.2 Choose a Budding Industry

When we explore the success ingredients of BYD, the first thing catching people's eye is the industries that BYD selected to enter. BYD's major business lines cross rechargeable batteries, new-energy-powered automobiles, and new energy industries which are all sunrise industries in China and in the world as well. In particular, the new-energy-powered automobile was the most notable one of BYD in the market today.

China's auto industry, generally speaking, is still in its fast development stage, and the demand for autos is still far away from the saturation point. At the same time, the domestic auto brands have been on the quick rise and their market shares have been noticeably increasing year over year. The auto production and sales in China was the largest in the world in 2010 with both production and sales exceeding 18 million units. The current vehicle population in China is around 114 million, which means that, on average, every one out of 12 persons owns a car. This number is still far below the level of the developed countries, and indicates great potential for auto industry in China in the future. The gradual formation and rise of China's domestic brands such as BYD, CHERY and GEELY broke the monopoly of the joint venture brands such as GM-Shanghai, and led the Chinese auto industry towards a new paradigm. According to the statistics of the CAAM, the sales of the domestic auto brands have reached 2.933 million and the market share of these brands was about 30.89 % in the year of 2010.[4] China's domestic auto makers have better understanding about the domestic customers' needs, more flexible design ability to accommodate customers' preferences, and stronger cost management, and thus play an increasingly important role in the market place. Domestic auto brand manufacturers, as represented by BYD, CHERY and GEELY, continuously increase their investments on R&D and product designs, and have significantly improved quality and functionality of their autos, gained higher degree of recognition from the market, and accelerated growth of their sales and market shares.

Energy saving and emission reduction have been commonly acknowledged in the car designs, and using new energy undoubtedly is the direction to go for the further development of auto industry. Ever since 2008, how to develop new-energy-driven automobile has become the focus of the entire global auto industry with the increased pressure of the soaring oil price, the energy saving and emission reduction. In order to make the strategic transition for its growth model, the

[4] http://www.caam.org.cn/newslist/a35-1.html

Chinese government issued a series of policies to support the new-energy-driven cars. The auto industry has been listed as one of the strategic emerging industries in China's long term plan. For example, in June 2012, the China's State Council released "The 12th Five-Year Plan for National Strategic Emerging Industries". According to this plan, the new energy auto industry will accelerate the R&D on its core technologies and applications to enhance the industry integration. As announced by China's Ministry of Finance, they plan to inject about 1–2 billion RMB every year into new-energy-driven auto industry and remove all the restrictions on license plate auction, license-plate lottery and traffic control with new-energy-driven cars. These policy supports and the awareness of general public about energy conservation and emission reduction will undoubtedly drive the development of the new-energy-driven auto in China into a new stage.

According to a forecast issued by IIT in Japan, the sales of electric cars, hybrid cars and plug-in hybrid cars will reach 4 million units in 2015, and 8 million in 2020. In addition, according to a recent research report issued by the China Academy of Science and Technology for Development,[5] the ownership of pure electric cars and plug-in hybrid cars in China can rise to above 0.5 million by 2015, the moderate/heavy hybrid cars can approach 1 million and the average fuel consumption of the passenger cars will be reduced to 5.9 l/100 km, and the power battery production capacity can be nearly 10 billion watts. By 2020, the ownership of pure electric cars and plug-in hybrid cars can grow to 5 million units, sales of moderate/heavy hybrid cars will account for 50 % of the sales of passenger cars, the domestic automobile fuel efficiency can meet the international standard, and the average fuel consumption of the passenger cars will approach 4.5 l/100 km. Such huge new-energy-driven auto market will become the determining factor for the auto companies in competing for their market positions.

Meanwhile, long term demand for electric cars is projected to keep growing with focus on the second- and third-tier cities in China. Alike to the auto industry's development in Japan and Korea in the past, it's quite promising for China's auto market to remain fast growing in the next 3–5 years along with the high economic growth in China. Considering the large population and low ownership per family in China, the forecasted growth rate of automobile sales can reach 10 % in the next 10 years.[6]

However, there are some downsides as well for the auto industry in terms of strict regulations and control on the entry permit, investment, production and sales for the auto industry in China. On one hand, the development policy of automobile industry enacted by China's National Development and Reform Committee (NDRC) has clearly stipulated that the initial investment of an automobile factory should be above RMB 2 billion, the investors' own fund should be no less than RMB 800 million, and the R&D investment could not be less than RMB 500 million. Such huge capital requirement is the main barrier for the new entries.

5 http://www.casted.org.cn/en/web.php?NewsID=5327

6 http://auto.sohu.com/20120712/n348008224.shtml

On the other hand, the economy of scale plays an important role in the auto industry, and it won't be profitable until a certain level of scale is achieved. Therefore, it is usually difficult for a new company to be able to conduct large-scale production and secure the operation funds from day one. In addition, there is also high requirement for the technology used, and a company may be stuck in an unfavorable situation if it lacks independent research ability and its core technology.

## 2.3 All Movement Starts with Power

Even though BYD is best known today for its new-energy-powered cars, its initial business line is rechargeable batteries. The market share of the rechargeable batteries that were made domestically in China has been sustainably growing during the last several years. Currently, the rechargeable batteries are widely used in the cell phones, laptops, electric tools and other electronic products. More specifically, lithium Ion battery has been utilized in mobile phones, laptops and digital cameras, and nickel cadmium battery has been installed in the electric tools and electric toys. Of course, the largest application of rechargeable battery is still the cell phone.

At present, the rechargeable batteries are primarily produced in China, Japan and Korea. The major producers are Sanyo Electric, SONY and Panasonic in Japan, and Samsung and LG in Korea. The companies in China, Japan and Korea pretty much dominate the entire lithium Ion battery market worldwide. In addition to BYD, there are also some other producers in the Chinese domestic market, such as China Bak Battery, Tianjin Lishen Battery and Dongguan New Energy. As the competition intensified, the market share of Japanese producers has been diminishing while China and Korea's shares have been on rise.

The industry's entry threshold, however, has been elevated due to the technology upgrade and increased scale of production. The rechargeable batteries require high technologies which are needed to ensure the stability and energy density for battery products. At present, some core technologies can only be developed by BYD and few large companies in Japan and Korea. New entrants are confronted with big obstacles if they don't have the access to such key technologies.

Moreover, it is often those large-scaled electronic product companies that are the buyers of the rechargeable batteries as well, and they typically demand high quality for the batteries. The supplier can obtain the opportunity to provide such high quality products with low cost only if they have large-scaled production and possess fine quality control system. Therefore, the new entrants will find it even harder to break into the current market.

Fast development of the downstream industry and stable increase of demand for rechargeable battery is the trend in the current rechargeable battery industry. Many portable electronic devices such as mobile phones, personal computers, digital cameras, digital video cameras and MP3 have gradually become parts of consumers' daily life, and lithium-ion battery has been gradually adopted in these electronic products. As a result, the demand for lithium-ion battery has been increasing significantly. Meanwhile, the market share of NI-MH battery and nickel–cadmium cell has been decreasing due to the low energy density. However, the NI-MH battery market share remained stable due to the demand from the hybrid cars. In addition, the government policy supports towards the new-energy-driven automobiles will further increase the demand of rechargeable battery including NI-MH battery, because such battery serves a critical role for new-energy-driven cars.

More specifically, there are three factors that BYD's rechargeable batteries powered the success of BYD's car business. The first one is BYD's independent research that enabled BYD to develop the lithium iron phosphate battery, which is a safer, greener, longer lasting, and less expensive technology with a technical advantage over the NI-MH battery in the operation of hybrid electric vehicles (HEV) in terms of energy density, power generating, discharge rate, and the improvement in the acceleration performance, maximum speed and endurance of cars. At present, BYD has more than 100 lithium iron phosphate battery patents and more than 90 patent applications.

The second one is the better power generator for the electric vehicle that BYD produced. The permanent magnet synchronous motor (PMSM) developed by BYD has bigger power, torque, and lower weight-to-power ratio, with productivity of 5–60 kw, which can completely meet the requirements of dual-mode electric vehicles and Blade Electric Vehicles (BEV).

The third one is the synchronized power control system. The integrated power control system of BYD matches power cell, driving motor and the whole vehicle system all together. This system combines the hybrid mode and the EV mode, and, in this way, the goal of "going green and environment protection" is also achieved in the sense that cars may only rely on the battery when the cell is full. When battery is low, however, it will be switched to the hybrid mode and the fuel efficiency is also raised.

## 2.4 The Energy of New Energy Industry

At the same time, many attentions have been given to the clean or alternative energies in general. Concerning on the non-reproducible nature of the existing energies and environment protection, many countries are looking for a solution of renewable energy for sustainable economic growth. Solar energy came into people's attention and got increasing policy support because of its abundance, even distribution and cleanliness. In addition, it requires relatively low initial investment, and is closer to the end users, which helps solve the problems caused by the long distance transmission, lower the operating cost, and increase the transmission efficiency. Therefore, solar energy has become one of the major trends of future energy development in the world, including China.

Technically, however, the solar and wind types of energy cannot be integrated directly to the traditional power grid due to their highly dependence on the environment and unstable power. For this reason, electric-power storage stations can help smooth the electricity power provision of solar energy and solve the issue of instability. In addition, the electric-power storage station can store the energy surplus and release them when there is a need or shortage. This functionality of electric-power storage station can adjust and iron out the "peaks and troughs" in the electricity demand curve.

According to a forecast released by Pike Research, the market scale of energy storage stations will increase from USD $1.5 billion in 2010 to $35.3 billion in 2020.[7] With the development of the new-energy-generated electricity and smart grid, the large scale of commercial application of the electric-power storage station will be accelerated, and this will greatly enhance the development of the new rechargeable batteries represented by the iron cell. According to the data provided by the European Photovoltaic Industry Association (EPIA), the installed capacity of solar energy reached 7,203 MW in 2009, and will reach 0.3 billion MW in 2014, and the sales revenue of solar energy battery will attain $165 billion in 2015.[8]

Holding the core technology and well maintained government relationship, BYD has become the leader in the new energy industry in China by making great effort and progress in the new energy automobiles, solar energy and electric-power storage stations.

The key for new energy vehicle is the battery which is also one of the most important factors that customers are concerned on new energy vehicle. The competition of new energy vehicles boils down to the competition of the batteries. However, BYD started the R&D on battery technology very early and gained tremendous early comer advantages. BYD is now a leading electric vehicle maker in the entire world. In 2008, BYD introduced the hybrid car F3DM which was the first model not relying upon the professional charging stations, and electric car E6 and electric bus K9 appeared later. BYD's good government relationship also helped BYD promote and commercialize its electric vehicles successfully. In 2010, BYD sold 1,000 K9 electric bus to Changsha municipal government. In addition, in 2011, BYD signed a memorandum of understanding (MOU) with the SMRT Corporation in Singapore, which manages public transportation of Singapore, for further cooperation in the electric buses and taxies, and an agreement with the DAN Bus Company in Israel to replace the half of its current operating vehicles with BYD's electric bus, which is also the first time for Israel to have the full-sized electric bus. What's more is that the BYD's E6 pure electric taxi running in Shenzhen has very good performance. On average, every E6 car has been

[7] Pike Research: http://finance.21cn.com/newsdoc/zx/a/2013/0204/08/20343293_all.shtml

[8] EPIA: http://www.epia.org/home/

running over 1 year and 100,000 km without any technical defects and the quality of battery has been tested to be highly stable and reliable. Motivated by the maturing technology, abundant government subsidies, and the establishment of the charging facilities, the electric vehicle industry starts to grow fast, and BYD is undoubtedly the largest beneficiary.

Solar energy is another revenue engine for BYD in its initial field—rechargeable battery industry. BYD has established a vertical integration of business lines including poly-silicon, Silicon chip, battery module and packaging. BYD entered into the solar industry in October 30, 2008 by taking the Solar Cell Project from the Shangluo municipal government in Shanxi province. This is a multi-phased construction program for an annual productivity of 1 GW poly-silicon and 1 GW solar energy. In the first phase of project, BYD had achieved the annual output of 100 MW poly-silicon and 100 MW solar energy in 2010, and in phase two, it had realized the annual output of 300 MW in 2011. So far, the annual output has risen to 600 MW and the ultimate goal is to reach 1 GW annually. The businesses of solar cells and parts have brought revenue of RMB 759 million to BYD. For any solar energy companies, the core competence would be the energy conversion efficiency and the conversion cost. As for the energy conversion efficiency, BYD has a leading edge of 16.5 % of efficiency in the world. Then, for the conversion cost, BYD adopted the metallurgical method instead of the traditional Siemens process.[9] This helps BYD lower down its cost by 20 %. With the superiority in cost and efficiency, solar cell has become the important cash cow of BYD.

BYD also did well in the electric-power storage stations. The iron cell of BYD has an advantage over those traditional lead acid batteries in that iron cells have high-power charge–discharge property and avoid the problem of instability of wind energy and solar energy. BYD got the pilot project to build up the electric-power storage stations and the energy conversion system for the China Southern Power Grid Co. in August 2010. Later, BYD started cooperation with the Los Angeles Department of Water and Electricity (LADWP) in the project to develop the renewable electricity power grid in September 2010. BYD also signed a contract with the Changsha municipal government for a project of a 10 MW electric-power storage station. With the support of the various level of government in and outside China, BYD made the steady progress in the commercialization of electric-power storage stations.

[9] Siemens process referred to a popular process based on the thermal decomposition of trichlorosilane at 1100 °C on a heated silicon rod placed inside a deposition chamber. This process was developed in the late 50s with reference to the company that carried out its early development and was abandoned recently due to its high energy consumption and pollution.

## 2.5 Money Is Power, Too

BYD became notable not only because it developed a new type of physical power to energize new types of automobiles and new electronics, but also it presented to the business community and beyond a great example to utilize the financing to "power" its success.

In addition to its historical listing HK Stock Exchange in 2002 with HK$1.6 billion raised, which significantly consolidated BYD's leading position in the battery industry, and provided BYD with the opportunity to enter the auto industry, BYD also conducted pre-IPO financing to make BYD not only technically ready for taking-off, but also financially ready for getting access to the public funding to support its business expansion.

At the end of August 2008, Warren Buffett was interviewed by "Squawk Box" of CNBC and told interviewer that "You will see me making abundant investment in China in favorable environment." Following his talk soon, on September 27, 2008, Buffett's Sino-American Energy Holdings Co. announced buying the shares of BYD. Sino-American spent $230 million for buying 225 million shares of BYD, which account for 10 % of the entire BYD outstanding shares.

Buffet's PE equity financing is critical for BYD's next step development and eventual success. It was not difficult to figure out the decline of the traditional auto industry then and the key for the future development lies in the new-energy-powered automobiles. Not only these new types of automobiles are the solution to the energy safety and environmental protection, but also it represents future cash cow of the industry. Those who can secure their market positions today will have much better chance to earn a higher return in the future.

However, the issue is that it will typically take a really long time to see pay-off for the investment on new-energy-driven vehicles, while the R&D on new-energy-driven vehicles usually requires a huge amount of funds. Without sufficient capital and technological innovation ability, the chance for failure is high in terms of either R&D, or the commercialization of the innovation. Moreover, back in 2008, the infrastructure for electricity charge stations in China was not in place yet, and these new-energy-driven automobiles were just scraps.

However, BYD's financing ability by getting the favor of Buffett totally changed the game. Buffet's injection of his PE equity fund helped BYD obtain the money needed for R&D, and also made BYD ready for its later gaining the access to the public funding. Since then, everything happened in BYD was considered to be aligned with the expectations. BYD's stock price soared for almost ten times in 2009. The USD $230 million of Buffett's investment rose to $2.3 billion and Chuangfu Wang became the richest man of the year in China.

In addition, a strategic investor such as Warren Buffett not only brought BYD with financing, but also generated great branding effect for BYD. With Buffet's investment, BYD was known by the whole world overnight. To help BYD gets publicized, Buffett even recommended BYD's electro mobiles to President Obama of United States. This "soft power" truly energized BYD for its full speed journey.

## 2.6 Innovation through Imitation

The success of BYD was also largely attributed to its "imitation-based innovation" model advocated by Chuanfu Wang. As a CEO with engineer background, Wang requested that all the engineers of BYD should learn how to dissemble cars first, and BYD even allocates a budget for purchasing these best designed and made cars such as Benz, BMW and Toyota for the engineers to dissemble, imitate, and then, possibly innovate. During the course, BYD tried all possible ways to legally follow the patent protection requirements.

Facing the questions regarding whether BYD was actually just a copying cat, Chuanfu Wang responded in the following way. It seems to him that, for any creation of a new product in this world, 60 % is based on public literature, 30 % on existing samples, the 5 % is on material factors, and only 5 % comes from an independent R&D. BYD adopted many non-patent technologies and how to mix these non-patent technologies became BYD's innovation. Patents should be respected but the dispute for patent issue could be legally resolved. It seems to him, the imitating-based innovation is not purely copying and it's legal.

Based on such a model, BYD has made a great breakthrough on the R&D and produced a car of model BYD-F3 that is the first model of entirely-domestic-made car with sales over 100,000 units in China. At the same time, this model significantly reduced the budget for R&D, and hence, reduced the production cost and made the car more affordable for more potential buyers.

## 2.7 The Vertical Integration of An Entire Industry Chain

BYD recognized that the imitation-based innovation may help BYD's growth to certain extent, but cannot help maintain their leading position in the market in the long run. As Chuangfu Wang stated, BYD's ultimate goal is to build an advanced R&D platform instead of merely imitating. Indeed, what truly helped build up BYD's leading position in the market place is its vertical integration across rechargeable batteries, new-energy-powered automobiles, and new energy industries based on their unique advantages in the battery technology.

BYD introduced the new hybrid car model F3DM to the market on December 15, 2008. F3DM was equipped with the "iron cell" which was independently developed by BYD with more than 700 patents that BYD has applied for. Such iron cell was widely considered a great technology breakthrough, and that's also one of the reasons why many global companies haven't made significant progress in the electro-mobile industry yet, simply because they haven't developed such advanced batteries.

To the investors, the true attractiveness of BYD is its leading position in several important new-energy-related industries through the vertical integration based on its advanced battery technology. Rupert Hoogewerf[10] once said, Chuangfu Wang follows the trend in scientific and technology development, innovation in new energy, and the rising environmental concerns, and thus, created a new pattern in the auto industry.

Furthermore, the BYD's vertical integration covers a whole industry chain including energy generation, collection, transportation, charging, electro mobile parts, and electro mobiles. According to a forecast issued by the World Bank,[11] the market value for the entire automobile chain can reach USD $280 billion by 2020—a very promising future for the companies in the industry. And currently, BYD is the only auto company who has integrated the whole industry chain.

## 2.8 Can BYD Continue Its Legacy?

BYD's core business lines consist of automobiles, rechargeable batteries and new energies. As for the automobile industry, as the development of new-energy-powered vehicles is heavily dependent upon the build-up of charging stations and the government's subsidies, so the new-energy-powered cars may not be able to be popular in a large scale in the next 3–5 years. Regarding the traditional-energy-powered car business, the second and third tier cities in China will become the main growing markets in the near future. One of the features of this market is its high level of sensitivity to price, which is definitely a piece of good news to BYD, because BYD can offer cars with a very affordable price and high performance-to-price ratio. Consequently, the key to capture such market is to design a variety of different car models and increase the performance ratio.

On the other hand, the new-energy-driven vehicles have gained increased attentions of the Chinese government, as China has started some quite generous subsidy policies to stimulate the purchase of new-energy-driven vehicles. It is expected that China's accumulative electric and hybrid vehicles will reach 500,000 units by 2015 and 5 million by 2020. As of June 2010, China's central government has launched trial subsidy programs in five Chinese cities—Shanghai, Changchun, Shenzhen, Hangzhou and Hefei. The program offers a subsidy of up to RMB 60,000 (about USD $9,523.2) to buyers of purely electric vehicles and RMB 50,000 to hybrid vehicle buyers. As a result, with the advanced technology and well-maintained government relationship, BYD's future in new-energy-driven vehicle business seems promising.

As for the rechargeable battery business, even though the sales revenue of BYD's rechargeable batteries has displayed some downturn recently due to the

---

[10] Rupert Hoogewerf, born in Luxembourg, is the publisher of the Hurun Report, a monthly magazine best known for its "China Rich List", a ranking of the wealthiest individuals in China. As a qualified chartered accountant, Hoogewerf worked for 7 years at Arthur Andersen, before launching Hurun Report.

[11] The China New Energy Vehicles Program: Challenges and Opportunities, World Bank, 2012.

revenue reduction of its customer companies that generally purchase batteries as part of their end product purchase from BYD, the sales of lithium battery used in new-energy-driven vehicles and other usages of the batteries are expected to drastically increase in the future.

However, the most promising business of BYD seems in the solar energy field. Because of its advantages in the R&D and manufacturing, BYD will be able to expand its solar business to the downstream power stations and establish a comprehensive photovoltaic power chain. Given its combined expertise in PV power station and storage, BYD can provide comprehensive on- and off-grid solutions in various markets of power storage.

As the first decade of the twenty-first century has revealed, this century will be a century that are featured by significant technology innovations, including the ones in the new energies that will power and shape our daily life for the rest of this century and beyond. Either by his vision, insight, or purely luck, Mr. Wang and BYD has occupied a very strategically advantageous spot that will allow BYD to fully capture all the potentials that the century will bring to a firm. To run a successful business in China today, one needs to have several ingredients of success in hand: low cost, high technology, adequate capital, industry integration, well maintained government relations, and powered by new energy. As the story told in this chapter, BYD is lucky enough to have them all. Therefore, it should be reasonable to trust Warren Buffet's judgment, as proved by the majority of his previous decisions, and project BYD with an even more gloried future.

# Chapter 3
# Urban Mining: The Story of GEM

**Abstract** This chapter discusses the case of GEM, a leading company in China's recycling industry. As China's fast economic growth generates tremendous demand for many non-renewable metals such as cobalt and nickel, of which China has limited reserves, GEM developed technologies and a business model that allow it to capture these opportunities in the recycling industry through a process they coined as "urban mining"

**Keywords** Recycling industry · Cobalt and nickel · Rechargeable batteries · Circular economy

"Urban mining"? Is that referring to a city built on metal mines? Or digging holes on city streets to explore metals underneath? Turns out, it's neither! The term was actually coined by a company called GEM in China's recycling industry in reference to the act of recycling cobalt and nickel from used materials such as retired equipment and machinery, or even from used consumer products that contain relevant metal elements. China's fast economic development has created an increasingly large gap between the needs from economic growth and amount supplied of various metals that China's natural environment lacks. The recycling of these scarce materials has not only become critical for the sustainability of China's continued growth, but also flourished as a market, generating tremendous values for the involved companies, their investors, and all related industries. As a quite representative case in this emerging industry in China, the ingredients of GEM's success in this widely concentrated industry, and business models developed by GEM that enabled the firm to "mine" scarce metals from urban areas would be intriguing to be dug out.

J. G. Wang and J. Yang, *Who Gets Funds from China's Capital Market?*,
SpringerBriefs in Business, DOI: 10.1007/978-3-642-44913-0_3, 

## 3.1 The Age of Recycling

It may be just unfortunate that the concept of modernization as defined or determined by the past few centuries is built so heavily upon the consumption of un-reproducible resources—oil, coal, and metals such as cobalt, nickel and others. It is just the inauspicious reality for our planet. While these resources have in fact helped create a world where the level of wealth and physical quality of life is higher than ever before, the sustainability of continuing on this current path is becoming one of the most hotly debated questions, as these un-reproducible resources get closer and closer to their residual values. The fundamental issue lies in this question: can the next generation, the next-next, and the dozens after that survive with the way we are living now?

In response to this worldwide challenge, both policy makers and business community are making great efforts to find creative solutions to meet this challenge, while simultaneously improving sustainability and generating tremendous value and opportunity for businesses that want to be in this game. It is a game where companies are competing with nature, time, for technological innovation; and, as an individual entity engaged, companies such as GEM are also competing on workable business models.

As of the mid-1980s, recycling cobalt and nickel resources has been listed officially on China's industry development agenda. According to the U.S. Geological Survey (USGS)[1], China's cobalt reserve base is about 73,300 tons, but the reserves that have economic values are only 40,900 tons, accounting for only 1.03 % of the world's economically viable cobalt reserves. Despite this scarcity China has a huge demand for cobalt at about 15,000 tons per year, which accounts for about 25 % of the world's total annual consumption.[2] This significant imbalance between demand and supply for cobalt forced China to become heavily dependent on imported cobalt. Therefore, if China is unwilling to rely so heavily on imported resources, it had no choice but to develop a recycling cobalt system and use renewable cobalt resources. The reality is, however, China's total renewable cobalt amounts to less than 2,000 tons per year, accounting for only 15 % of annual cobalt consumption.[3] While this apparent shortage represents a serious hurdle for China to overcome in its continued growth, it also provides an unprecedented opportunity to create a brand new industry around the recycling of scarce metals.

In addition to the cobalt shortage, China is also a country with a scarcity of nickel. The nickel reserve in China is about 2.32 million tons, only 3.56 % of world's total nickel reserves. If assuming an annual production of 210,000 tons a year as it was in 2007, all domestic reserve will be completely exploited in about

[1] http://www.usgs.gov/pubprod/data.html#data

[2] Demand and Supply of Cobalt around the world and in China, *Mining and Metallurgical Engineering*, 2012, 32(z1).

[3] All data of GEM are from the Prospectus of GEM unless indicated otherwise.

10 years. However, the good news is that, unlike recycled cobalt, recycled nickel has in rapid development worldwide in recent years, and its growth has even surpassed that of mined nickel. According to an industry resources report released by Antaike,[4] a consulting firm covering metal industries, the proportion of recycled nickel worldwide by 2003 had exceeded 30 % of the total global supply of nickel. There is further hope in that, in China, the recycling of nickel also saw remarkable growth. The issue at present is only with recycled nickel that is in its primitive forms, such as nickel salts or nickel iron. In addition, the price of nickel fluctuates frequently, bringing relatively low profits for nickel recycling companies. As a result, the decisive factors for growing the nickel recycling industry come down to the improvement of recycling technology and production at a higher end of industry value chain, so as to gain a higher added value of products.

## 3.2 Characteristics of the Recycled Cobalt and Nickels Industry

To better understand the background of GEM's rise, it may be beneficial to first take a look at some special features of recycled cobalt and nickels industry. What comes out first is its ***ever Increasing Demand.*** The growing demand for various resources in China, as driven by the fast economic growth, provides the cobalt-nickel recycling industry with plenty of space for development. According to estimates from Antaike, the consumption of cobalt powder in China will increase from 3,020 tons in 2008 to 4,330 tons in 2013, and the gap between the demand and the supply of cobalt powder in China will go from 2,400 tons to 3,130 tons by 2013. Similarly, with the development of powder metallurgy and the Ni-MH battery, the demand for nickel powder in China will also continue to grow. In 2013, the demand for nickel will be twice of that of 2008, and despite the increase of production capacity to 4,000 tons in 2013, the gap between demand and supply is still estimated to be as large as 4,050 tons.

Furthermore, the existing gap can't be simply fulfilled by imports, especially because the countries that export the two metals have begun to restrict their exports. Very soon, China will have no choice but to reduce its dependence on foreign suppliers. Given the limited reserves, however, the only option available to support China's rising demand would be to recycle cobalt and nickel, making quite certain that this industry will get strong backing from government policies, including potential funding support. Thanks to these conditions, cobalt and nickel recycling will definitely grow to be an industry with very promising prospects, and whoever catches this window opportunity will see their harvest soon down the road.

[4] Consulting Report of Cobalt & Nickel Industry, Antaike, 2010.

### 3.2.1 It's a Tech Game

The second feature of the recycling industry in China is its strong technological orientation. If the bar for entering into a promising industry is set too low, the profit margin of all companies involved will be dragged down almost instantaneously. Fortunately or unfortunately, the technical entry barrier of cobalt and nickel recycling industry has been significantly elevated in past years due to increased emphasis of government policies on environmental protection. In only a few years, the Chinese government had issued a slew of laws and regulations focusing singularly on the recycling industry and environmental protection, such as the Law on Promotion of Recycling Business, Management of Collection of Renewable Resources, and the Law on Prevention and Control of Environmental Pollution by Solid Wastes, all of which require that only companies that meet some pre-established standards are allowed to enter into the recycling business. And all these laws further mandate that all companies who want in on the recycling business have to go through a scrutiny and approval procedure.

In particular, because cobalt and nickel waste materials have the potential to pollute the environment, only the companies with the technology and capacity to operate without emitting contamination are allowed to engage in recycling cobalt and nickel wastes. In order to meet the quality requirements of the customers who use the recycled goods, the recycled products must possess the same quality as products made from originally mined material. These high bars of standard also effectively block many low quality recycled goods manufacturers, and prevent from the happening of what already happened in the lower end of the recycling market where the most companies can only produce the most primitive recycled products. As a leading firm in recycling technology, this effectively kept many potential competitors of GEM on the outside.

On a technical level, what GEM does is producing ultra-fine cobalt powder using cobalt waste, and the recycling technology it developed for extracting ultra-fine cobalt powder from discarded batteries, wasted catalysts and wasted hard alloys. Its manufacturing technology and product quality have all reached world standards. In terms of nickel, GEM independently developed a patent on chemical recovery technology, making it a pioneer in new technology in the industry. The updated technology marked the first time that a company has been able to mass-produce ultra-fine nickel powder without using the carbonyl or electrolysis methods. In fact, the production of ultra-fine nickel powder using GEM's technologies altered the landscape of the raw materials that qualified for nickel powder. Both the technologies developed for nickel and for cobalt have been certified by the Shenzhen Science and Technology Bureau, taking a leading position in Chinese technology and an advanced position worldwide. On top of that, GEM won the second ever Guangdong Science and Technology Achievement Award in 2007 for these patents.

### 3.2.2 *Rechargeable Batteries: The Source of Recycling Cobalt and Nickels*

The third feature is about the source of the recycling cobalt and nickels. As for "urban mining", a direct question is where to mine in an urban environment. The answer lies in discarded rechargeable batteries. Rechargeable batteries contain both cobalt and nickel, all of which can be recycled and "mined".

China is actually the largest producer and consumer of batteries in the world. Statistics show that the total domestic consumption of rechargeable batteries during 2001–2005 was 7.73 billion units. If assuming a three-year battery usage life and an average weight of 25 g for each Ni-Cd, Ni-MH or Lithium battery, then the total weight of all the discarded rechargeable batteries was 193,000 tons in just those 4 years. Out of those 193,000 tons, 32,900 tons were recyclable nickel, and 12,800 of recyclable cobalt.[5] The latter was equivalent to about 30 % of China's total reserve of mined cobalt at the time. If all those batteries were simply discarded and returned to nature through waste, they would have produced water pollution of 65 billion $m^3$, or the equivalent of 27,000 $km^2$ of lost ecological function in soil. Whether recycling nickel and cobalt from batteries is done for protection of the environment or for the fully utilization of scarce metal resources, there's no doubt that looking to discarded batteries is the right direction to go.

In accordance with this discovery, China's powerful central government agency, the National Development and Reform Commission (NDRC), listed the recycling of discarded batteries in the second batch of the recycling industry pilot program, and GEM itself was included in the list of pilot companies consigned to recycle the smaller grade of such discarded batteries. As research has gradually revealed, advanced recycling techniques of discarded batteries can largely improve recovery rate of precious metals, and lower production cost. Therefore, the discarded batteries provide a greater amount of raw materials for cobalt and nickel recycling companies, and will in turn increase their revenues and profits.

## 3.3 In China, You Never Have to Worry About Playing Alone

As is well known, in an efficient market, wherever there is an opportunity in terms of either demand or growth, there will be companies that rush into seize it. In China, however, even with a market that isn't fully efficient yet, you still never have to worry about playing the game alone. Given the country's 1.3 billion population, any Chinese company can be sure that it will always find itself

[5] Analyst Reports, China International Capital Corporation Limited, December 29th, 2010.

surrounded by more competitors than it could ever want. In this regard, the market for recycled cobalt and nickel products is no exception.

In China's cobalt and nickel recycling industry, there are numerous companies closely behind the leading companies such as GEM. Regions such as Qinghe of Hebei Province, Qingyuan of Guangdong Province, Taicang of Jiangsu Province, Linqu of Shandong Province, and Anhua of Hunan Province are nationwide collecting and distributing centers for cobalt and nickel waste. In Guangdong and Zhejiang Province, there are clusters of companies that recycle batteries containing cobalt and nickel through dismantling. However, Chinese companies and individuals such as these are mining the metals through very elementary processing techniques such as collecting and classifying wastes, and very few actually carry out the more intricate methods for processing cobalt and nickels needed in order to recycle large quantities of the metals.

In fact, GEM is the only company in China in this industry that has developed a series of patents and advanced techniques to recycle of cobalt and nickels, a result of the company's independent innovation. It has developed an advanced recycling process that turns cobalt and nickel wastes to ultra-fine cobalt and nickel powder, a process which utilizes the world's leading technologies and equipment. This leading edge in technology made GEM a very unique firm in the industry, and as of yet, no other Chinese company has been able to stand on equal footing.

### *3.3.1 A Leading Miner*

The growth of GEM is an integral part of the narrative of this industry. GEM, short for Green Eco-Manufacturer, was founded in December 28, 2001 in Shenzhen, Guangdong Province, and was restructured from a state-owned firm into a privately held company in December 2006. It successfully went public at Shenzhen Stock Exchange's Small and Medium Enterprise Board in January 2010 (SZSE stock code: 002340), and the first public company to engage in the activities of exploiting scarce metals from "urban mines", and also the first public company in the renewable resources industry and E-waste (electronic waste) recycling industry. GEM has now become the largest company in China to produce ultra-fine cobalt and nickel powder through the recycling of product wastes.

As the first Chinese company to initiate the idea of "Urban Mining" and introduce the concept of "Limited Resources, Unlimited Recycling" in China, GEM, in November 2011, was selected to be one of 60 "National Models of Circular Economy", because of their success in building an effective recycling system of E-waste and discarded batteries. In February 2012, GEM was appointed as one of the nine national circular economy education pilots, which made GEM the leader of China's recycling industry and a pioneer in low-carbon manufacturing. GEM has also become the face and name of China's circular economy, acting as a window through which the world can better understand China's environmental protection industry.

### 3.3.2 The Core Business of GEM

Specifically, GEM's core business is the recycling and re-utilizing of cobalt and nickel to produce ultra-fine cobalt and nickel powder. The final products are produced by using renewable resources that contain cobalt and nickel as raw materials, running them through recycling technologies that were independently developed by GEM. The high quality of these recycled products allows them to be direct substitutes for the metals that are mined from the earth. These products are widely used in fields such as hard alloy, battery materials, and powder metallurgy.

In recent years, the core business of GEM has been growing quickly. Though the prices of nonferrous metals continually went down in 2011, sales of GEM's major products still increased at 61.16 % on a year-over-year basis, realizing revenues of RMB 919 million a year. Gross profits amounted to RMB 133 million, which had grown by 37.16 %. Net profits available to shareholders were RMB 121 million, growing by 40.7 %. Finally, the earnings per share was RMB 0.49, growing by 36.11 %. The cobalt and nickel business generated a total income of RMB 560 million, accounting for 61.01 % of GEM's total sales revenue, while new businesses such as E-waste, WPC profiles and copper generated revenue of RMB 350 million, accounting for the rest 38.99 % of total revenue. The share of new businesses increased by 22 % points compared to 2010, and up by 9 % points compared with mid-2011.[6] The business of GEM had pretty much been driven by the double engines of cobalt/nickel products and E-waste recycling.

### 3.3.3 Parallel Circulation

If you are curious about the physical process of the cobalt and nickel recycling, you may want to read this section carefully. GEM, after collecting cobalt and nickel waste, uses recycling technologies such as originalization and remanufacturing to produce ultra-fine cobalt and nickel powders, which are then sold to downstream firms who use the powders to manufacture consumer goods such as batteries or alloy instruments. However, because the provider of wasted resources in the upstream is also the user of recycled products made by GEM in the downstream, the market structure of this recycling business is a circle, as illustrated in Fig. 3.1.

More than 90 % of the raw materials that GEM uses are various kinds of wasted cobalt and nickel material. The waste water and slag generated in recycling are circulated internally to the greatest extent possible. For the leftover that can't be recycled, GEM would be allowed to emit as much as would meet national emission standards. Outside of this quota, GEM would have to sign outsourcing disposal contracts with professional waste management companies in order to emit

6 Annual Report (2011), GEM.

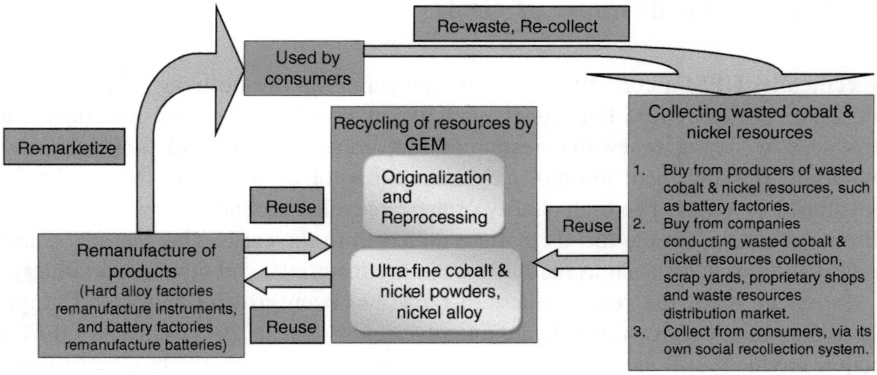


**Fig. 3.1** The circulation model of GEM in remanufacturing high-tech products from recycling wasted cobalt and nickel resources

the waste with treatment externally. This parallel model with both internal and external circulation is GEM's innovation, allowing wasted materials to be recycled without contamination and processed via high-tech resourcization.

### *3.3.4 High-End Recycled Products*

From a purely technical perspective, what distinguishes the recycling model of GEM from other recycling companies in China is that GEM adopts much more advanced technologies, and its ultra-fine cobalt and nickel powder is at the highest end of the value chain—hence, creating the highest added value for GEM. That is why GEM enjoys such high market share and handsome profitability, something that no other Chinese company in the industry has been able to even get close to.

As reported in the *Consulting Report of Cobalt & Nickel Industry* released by Antaike, the market share of GEM's products was in an upward trend from 2006 to 2008. Sales of cobalt powder increased from 6.65 to 15.56 %, up by 10 % points. Sales of nickel powder also increased from 2.5 to 4.5 %, almost twice as large before.

### *3.3.5 Growth through Funds*

In the age of monetary economy, a company can't grow without funding, and can't grow fast without external funding. Prior to receiving a bigger pool of funds from general public, however, it is necessary for a firm to first receive some pre-IPO investments to make the firm ready for public funding. Prior to their IPO, there were six rounds of capital injections and equity transfers, respectively, and GEM's largest shareholder was Huifengyuan, a company controlled by a couple, Kaihua Xu and Min Wang. Other shareholders were mainly institutional investors that were interested in GEM as it grew.

Among these investors, the most notable one is the second largest shareholder of GEM—Guangdong Science and Technology Venture Capital Co., Ltd (shortly, Guangdong VC). Guangdong VC is one of the oldest state-owned venture capital firms, one that gained a lot of public attention in the financial market due to its size of funds and the resources it receives from the government. On September 19, 2005, Guangdong VC became a shareholder when GEM transferred out parts of its equity for the third time, an act which also marked the first time that a VC/PE participated in the nonferrous metals industry in China. It was on that same day that another existing shareholder of GEM, Jingmen Yongfa, signed an Equity Transfer Agreement with Guangdong VC, Xiexun Industrials and Xu Kaihua, respectively. Through these transfers, Guangdong VC received 12 % equity of GEM.

Along with that interaction involving Jingmen Yongfa, Guangdong VC also separately transferred RMB 11 million into GEM's equity capital account. Within less than a year, in a second round of capital injection, Guangdong VC provided RMB 8 million of equity capital at a 1.25:1 ratio, with a premium for GEM's stocks worth RMB 6.4 million. At that point, Guangdong VC had contributed a total of RMB 21.64 million of equity capital to GEM. As GEM is also an important research incubator for Guangdong VC, the funds provided by latter played a pivotal role in the development of GEM at the early stage, and were also critical to GEM's survival through the 2008 financial crisis. It is indeed that Guangdong VC's funding gave GEM the opportunity to grow to the point that makes GEM ready for public funding.

In 2009, GEM went public by issuing 23.33 million A-shares of RMB denominated common stock in Shenzhen Stock Exchange (Ticker: 002340). These shares accounted for 25 % of post-IPO equity, and were set at an offering price of RMB 32 Yuan and a P/E ratio of 78.05, P/B ratio of 3.14. The total capital it raised was estimated at RMB 746.56 million, with a net capital of RMB 703 million.

## 3.4 The Right Thing at the Right Time

A number of "right" things that GEM did or several strategic decisions that GEM made right may contribute the success of GEM, such as:

### *3.4.1 Urban vs. Natural Mines*

GEM's exploitation of "Urban Mines" as raw materials for the recollection and recycling of metals gave GEM three major advantages over the companies that use natural mines to extract the same metals. First and foremost, "Urban Mines" rely on sources of used metal that are far more abundant than natural mines. Seeing as China is a country with scarce cobalt and nickel resources, and the few that do exist are primarily controlled by a select oligarchy, it's difficult to satisfy domestic demand by exploiting natural mines alone. If natural mines were the only sources of metal used, the supply of raw materials would be extremely unstable. For example, in 2007, as a result of the change in export polices by African countries, more than 60 % of the cobalt smelting factories in China were in the state of semi-shut down.

The second advantage of GEM's business model is that the exploitation of "Urban Mines" makes it easier for them to get support from the government. The Chinese government attaches great importance to the issue of resource shortage and environmental protection, and exploiting "Urban Mines" effectively reduces the pollution from wasted materials while cooperating with the social development theme of resources recycling. This doesn't just help GEM gain government's support, but also allows GEM to establish a good brand image in the minds of investors and consumers.

The third advantage is that the sources of "Urban Mining" are increasing. In December 2007, the National Development and Reform Commission and the Ministry of Environmental Protection approved GEM as a national pilot for the recycling of discarded batteries. From Shenzhen to Wuhan, this project publically and effectively promoted GEM's nationwide social recollection system for recycled cobalt and nickel resources, such as discarded batteries, which in turn ensured that GEM would be able to obtain a solid supply of nickel and cobalt resources in order to continue expanding the scale of their processing.

### *3.4.2 Replicating Success and Economies of Scale*

Compared to the fates of traditional recycling companies, GEM had demonstrated a strong capacity to operate away from their hometown. In the very beginning, GEM successfully built a "Recollection Model" in Hubei Province that integrated recycling bins and recycling supermarkets/3R shops and involved collaboration with waste resources suppliers; this model is also known as the "Wuhan Model". Since then the model has been replicated successfully in other places such as Shenzhen of Guangdong Province, Jingmen of Hubei Province, Fengcheng of Jiangxi Province, Wuhan of Hubei Province, and Wuxi of Jiangsu Province. GEM used this successfully transferrable model to develop a system of recycling production bases covering South, Central, East, North and Southwest China, allowing them to obtain stable inputs of waste resources.

For a company like GEM that uses "Urban Mines" as raw materials, the expansion of recollection channels is the foundation of rapid development, and the improvement of the recollection system can significantly lower costs. Since the waste resources collected by GEM's own recollection system only need to bear transportation costs and labor costs, which is significantly lower than the cost of operations of the recollection systems of other companies in the industry, the potential for expansion of this innovative recollection system forecasts even further cost savings in the future.

### *3.4.3 The Integration of Research, Innovation and Commercialization*

Under GEM's model, technology is the core. Only highly sophisticated technology will lead to the possibility of higher profits from higher value-added products. In order to obtain and develop such systems, GEM teamed up its company's engineers with university professors and well-equipped R&D labs and incubators, to ensure that it would have the technical capacity to compete with its competitors around the world. With a CNASCA (China National Accreditation Service for Conformity Assessment) national accredited lab and a public technology platform with CMA (China Metrology Accreditation), the R&D Center of GEM is also the support unit for the R&D center of Environmentally-Friendly Metals Engineering Technology in Shenzhen, and the R&D center of Secondary Nonferrous Metals Recycling Engineering Technology in Hubei Province. GEM's R&D Center had the high tech equipment and innovation capacity to conduct independent materials testing, performance evaluation and basic researches in-house. GEM has also undertaken more than 20 technological projects at national, provincial and municipal levels, including the famous State 863 Project, and it has won three Scientific and Technological Achievement Award at all three levels as well.

## 3.5 Exploring New Growth Areas

With the funding from the IPO, GEM's recycling industry value chain further expanded both in depth and breadth. Investment projects including the recycling of precious metals, wasted electrical appliances hardware and wasted plastics are all moving ahead of schedule. By the end of June 2012, 60 % of the total planned projects had been accomplished, and it was estimated that all of them would meet necessary standards for use. The E-waste recollection and recycling project was also estimated to meet usable standards by December 2013. The new business model for GEM will be one being driven by the double engines of cobalt/nickel products and E-waste recycling. While the cobalt and nickel business described through most of this case will continue to be the main source of the corporate top line, the recycling of E-waste will become a new growth spot for GEM for a number of reasons.

First, China is the world's largest manufacturer and consumer of household electrical appliances. In 2010, sales of televisions, washing machines, refrigerators, air conditioning and personal computers exceeded 6 billion unites. According to Japan's Fuji Economic Survey, in 2010, China's production of household electrical appliances was 85.3 % of the world's total amount in unit, and China's share of total sales revenue was 23.4 %, both of which ranked first globally. Thanks to the rapid development of China's economy and the continuous improvement of living standards, sales of household electrical appliances have been increasing at an annual growth rate of more than 20 % in the past 5 years. Assuming that the usage life of most general electrical appliances is 10–15 years, China will have begun to enter the peak period of E-waste as of this year, generating annual waste of over 50 million units, with waste growing at an annual rate of 20 %. Despite the huge market, however, due to the strict environmental standards and technical entry barrier, only few companies may be able to enter into this industry to compete with GEM. Thus, this line of business brings to GEM a bright prospect.

Secondly, the E-waste recycling business has both great environmental value and huge economic value. E-wastes contain a lot of reusable resources such as steel, nonferrous metals and plastics. An analysis by UBS shows that from 1 ton of arbitrarily collected circuit boards, one can extract 286 pounds of copper, a pound of gold, 44 pounds of tin and heavy metals including lead, cadmium and nickel.[7] The amount of these metals found in recycled electronics surpasses even the amount minable from natural ores. E-waste is therefore a valuable source of raw materials that have huge economic value. For GEM, this is all a virtuous cycle—the environmental and economic value generated from the E-waste recycling business will enable GEM to receive more support from government policies and subsidies.

In addition, in the last 2 years, GEM newly enabled their recollection production lines to extend to multiple metals including copper, aluminum, wolfram, iron, gold, silver, platinum and palladium. In particular, this system has added 30 tons of processing capacity to GEM's technologies, allowing them to process E-wastes such as wasted circuit boards in order to recycle rare precious metals of high value. The project of recycling rare precious metals has been moving along as planned. By the end of June 2012, GEM had accomplished 60 % of total undertaking projects, and it was estimated that these projects will contribute more profit for the company in the second half year of 2012.

This new development was also reflected financially in GEM's financial reports of 2011 and the first half of 2012. It showed that GEM was able to ensure the stable development of its recycling of cobalt and nickel wastes, and, simultaneously, the new businesses have brought along with them new spots of growth and profitability. In the first half of 2012, whereas the revenue from traditional cobalt and nickel business was stable with a year-on-year increase of 6.22 %, new

[7] See Analysis Report of GEM, UBS Securities, August 4th, 2011.

businesses such as E-wastes, WPC profiles, and copper and wolfram contributed to 46 % of GEM's total revenue. When the newly added project of tungsten carbide was officially put into operation, it generated sales of RMB 84.02 million, leading to an increase of 114 % in non-core business revenues.

## 3.6 Looking Forward

Since GEM got involved with E-wastes recycling, the proportion of ultra-fine cobalt and nickel powder in total revenue and gross profit has been declining. However, it still remains at above 80 % of GEM's total revenue and profit, and remains a core component of GEM's business model. GEM is continuously expanding and deepening its major businesses. In 2012, GEM acquired KLK (Jiangsu Cobalt & Nickel Metal Co., Ltd) so that in the long run, GEM has the potential to reach new heights in the cobalt industry.

KLK is China's top-ranked brand in the rechargeable battery recycling industry for cobalt and positive electrode materials—specifically, KLK are known for producing cobalt tetroxide and their sophisticated technology, stable market share, and market influence at home and abroad. The acquisition of KLK will expand GEM's production scale of cobalt, solidify its position in China's cobalt industry, and open the door to an international market. KLK is also a main shareholder of Seimi Tongda, which produces positive electrode materials. Therefore, the acquisition integrates the whole industry value chain for cobalt—battery—cobalt recycling, and wasted cobalt and nickel can be used as substitutes of natural mined cobalt after recycling. GEM will be able to gain an advantageous position in the market through its recollection channels and recycling technologies, allowing their "traditional" business to still remain its main source of revenue.

At the same time, GEM intends to seriously pursue a fast expansion of a production line of rare precious metals (i.e., gold and silver). Their involvement in wolfram and cooper recycling has also helped strengthen GEM's position as a leader in the recycling industry.

Finally, frequently-issued government policy support and the huge size of the renewable resources market provide a bright outlook for GEM's medium-term profit. The large-scale disposal of E-waste fits into trending concepts such as the "circular economy" and "resources recycling" that are strongly advocated by the state, and the gradual integration of the recycling industry chain is sure to unify the positive economic and social benefits. Moreover, since GEM's E-waste recycling model is very mobile and easily transferrable to different locations, it will be relatively cheap for GEM to pursue cross-region expansions and enhance their brand image, social perception and technological know-how. As UBS Securities estimates, the growth of GEM's net profit in the next few years will be maintained at approximately 30 %. A very promising future for GEM is down the road for the years to come.

# Chapter 4
# Moving Towards New Agriculture: The Story of Western Animal Husbandry

**Abstract** The Melamine scandal of 2008 resulted in the crisis of the century for the dairy industry in China. The imbalance of soaring demand for dairy products and lack of large-scaled animal husbandry farms led to the creation of thousands of small and remotely-located farms in order to fill the demand gap. This system, however, generated a sequence of food safety issues in the industry process. Western, a leading animal husbandry company discussed in this chapter, developed a successful business model that tackled the issue of quality while ensuring profitability.

**Keywords** Dairy industry · Animal husbandry industry · Melamine scandal · Decentralized standardization · Industry value chain

The Melamine scandal in 2008 truly resulted in the crisis of the century for the dairy industry in China.[1] The scandal officially broke on July 16, 2008 after 16 infants in Gansu Province—who had been fed milk powder produced by Shijiazhuang-based Sanlu Group—were diagnosed with kidney stones. After the initial focus on Sanlu—a market leader in the budget segment—government inspections found that the same problem also existed, just in slightly lesser degrees, in the products of 21 other dairy companies, including some well-known domestic brands such as Mengniu, Yili, and Yashili. Without question, as a result of this scandal, the dairy companies in the upstream of the industry, whose primary business is raw and fresh milk production, suffered a heavy blow. They would spend the next many years tackling the enormous challenge of regaining consumer confidence and rebuilding creditability, not just as individual companies but for the industry as a whole. Simply adapting the more advanced western model of large-scale cultivation, however, may not be possible for China in the short-term due to the natural environment requirements and the enormous investment necessary to implement the system. Fortunately, Animal Husbandry in West China developed a unique way of transformation of China's dairy industry based on China's local situation. Let's take a close look in the following sections to see what they did and how they did it.

---

[1] http://baike.baidu.com

J. G. Wang and J. Yang, *Who Gets Funds from China's Capital Market?*,
SpringerBriefs in Business, DOI: 10.1007/978-3-642-44913-0_4, 

## 4.1 Raw Milk: An Industry in Chaos

As part of the new agricultural lifestyle in modern day China, animal husbandry has become an important part of consumers' daily life. Meat, poultry, eggs, and dairy products serve as major sources of protein in the everyday diet of modern Chinese. Among these animal products, milk has the highest nutritional value. Since the year 1978, when China started its reform in opening up to trade and exchange to foreign countries, the nation has witnessed a rapid development of the dairy industry including a dramatic increase in the number of dairy cows, milk production, and dairy products. Because of the steady growth of dairy product consumption, China has become the third largest country in milk production in the world, following closely after America and India. However, even though there was a big increase in the overall volume of dairy product consumption, the consumption per capita is only about 25.2 kg per year, which is about 1/4 of the entire world's average consumption level and 1/12 of the per capita consumption in developed countries.[2] According to statistics, a 10 % increase in income will result in a 0.32 % increase of consumption in dairy. Because China on the whole has seen a rise in income, the country has also seen milk products become a daily necessity for rural and urban Chinese, especially as a critical source for protein. As income rises further, consumption is certain to increase as well. This change points to long-term growth potential for the dairy industry in China, and also for the closely associated animal husbandry industry.

The development of animal husbandry, however, does place high requirements on natural environment, not only needing large amounts of pasture, but also a certain level of technical know-how on the part of the farmlands. Take the breeding of dairy cows for example: dairy farms are usually located in the easy-to-isolate higher ground in order to block off pollutants. Usually, this means areas with relatively less human activity and sources of pollution.

In order to build large scale farms, environmental requirements for the breeding of dairy cows must be satisfied. Because of these requirements, modern animal husbandry areas are restricted to only a few large pastoral areas. The Fig. 4.1 shows the current geographic allocations of the milk production as well as animal husbandry in China.

Traditionally, Inner Mongolia, Xinjiang, and Heilongjiang provinces are the areas that provide superior natural conditions for animal husbandry. The milk produced in Xinjiang and Inner Mongolia are famous for their high quality.

The Western Animal Husbandry company discussed in this chapter is a part of the raw milk industry. Because it is a necessity in consumers' daily lives, milk has very low consumption elasticity, and does not fluctuate as the business cycle does.

[2] All data about Western Husbandry and dairy industry are from Initial Public Offering Prospectus of Western Animal Husbandry, unless indicated otherwise.

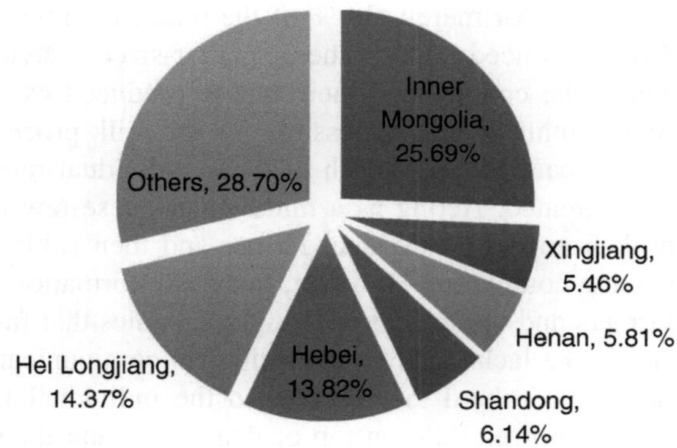


**Fig. 4.1** Distribution of animal husbandry in China. *Data source* Prospectus of Xinjiang Western animal husbandry Co. Ltd

In the eyes of industry outsiders, the profits from the milk business seem to be very high, but in reality, most profits are taken primarily by milk processing companies, and only very little is left for the upstream raw milk firms. This causes the distribution of profit in the dairy industry in China is extremely unbalanced. In the vertical chain of the dairy industry, the ratio between the investments allocated to cow breeding, milk products processing and sale of milk products is 7.5/1.5/1, but the corresponding profit ratio is 1/3.5/5.5.[3] The production process of raw milk requires the highest level of investment but receives the lowest profit and is exposed to the highest level of risk. This unbalanced cost/benefit schedule for the upstream versus the downstream of the dairy industry chain has already exerted negative impact on the sustainability and healthy, stable development of the industry, and contributed to many social issues such as the Melamine scandal in 2008.

Melamine is a chemical material with low toxicity, but excessive intake of melamine can lead to severe health problems such as kidney stones. But why was there excessive melamine in the milk produced by over 20 of China's domestic brands? It became clear that the cause was neither a result of accident or carelessness. After some inspection, the state inspection agency found that melamine had been routinely added by cow farmers and milk stations to the raw milk collection process so that the protein content would reach industry standard, bringing about much lower costs. Such a scandal was not only an indication of the lack of morality of some of these unlawful milk collection stations, it also reflected the chaotic situation of the raw milk supply chain and lack of effective supervision of the dairy industry in China.

Before the outbreak of the scandal, there were typically two types of raw milk suppliers: small-scaled dairy farmers and large-scaled farms. Using 20 cows as the cut-off point between "small" and "large" farms, the milk from large-sized farms

[3] "The emerging problems, solutions and prospects for the animal husbandry in China", *Agriculture Outlook*, 2008, 4th edition.

accounted for merely 30 % of the total raw milk supply, while the smaller-sized farms produced 70 %.[4] These smaller-sized individual cow farmers live scattered across the country and their supply produced by each individual farm was relatively small. It was impossible for the milk processing companies to collect raw milk separately from each of those individual farmers, and so raw milk stations were created. Acting as a middleman, these raw milk stations collected the raw milk from each individual farmer and then sold the collected milk to milk processing companies. However, there is information asymmetry between individual farmers and the milk processing companies that favors the processing companies, and also a lack of direct and sufficient communication between them. In addition, raw milk is hard to preserve, so the individual farmers don't have strong bargaining power. Add on top of that loose industry regulation and all these factors eventually provided raw milk stations a kind of monopsony position in the raw milk collection process. According to a report from the Renmin University's China-LyLe Milk Research Center,[5] the feedstock price had increased by more than 30 % and corn price more than 40 % in August, 2007 when compared to 1 year ago, and even indirect costs such as fuel price and land price had also risen. The raw milk price, however, had gone up by merely 3 % over that of that same period of time. The stagnating growth in the industry put pressure on the profits of the upstream supply chain companies, resulting in compounded pressure to the downstream companies. Some of these smaller sized individual farmers reacted to this pressure by lowering the quality of product through the addition of chemical protein additives.

While the supervision of the dairy industry in China is certainly deserving of reprimand, it should be said that it is in fact difficult to supervise such a vast system of wide-spread milk stations, especially if we're looking at it from a purely technical and logistical perspective. Meanwhile, even though there is a large demand for milk in China due to its large population, it is not feasible to simply adopt the large-scaled animal husbandry model used in the foreign countries, primarily for two reasons. First, foreign models of milk production require a huge amount of investment that may not be available in the short-term for China. Second, it will squeeze the profit margins of smaller sized farmers even further and may drive small-sized individual farmers out of business in mass. Considering these factors, the Chinese government suggested some policy supports for a parallel development strategy: the gradual development of the large-scaled animal husbandry farms, and technical support for the smaller sized individual farmers. For the large farms, the central government will encourage for an increase and expansion by providing the appropriate subsidies for the construction of water and electricity system, waste treatment system, epidemic prevention system, milking

[4] New Challenge and Solutions toward China's Milk Industry, *Agriculture Outlook*, Vol. 4, 2008.

[5] New Problems, Solutions and Trends in China's Milk Industry, *Agriculture Outlook*, Vol. 4, 2008.

facilities, forage and feedstock centers and other facilities. Meanwhile, the local government will set up the corresponding plans and allocate the land for cow breeding. For the smaller farms, the government will encourage some animal husbandry enterprises to provide cultivation techniques to the smaller-sized individual farmers, set up some professional organizations of the farmers such as cow farmer co-ops, and milk caw associations. The Western Animal Husbandry timely caught this window opportunity to develop a business model that greatly benefit from these government supporting policies.

## 4.2 Western's Journey of Growth

Western Animal Husbandry Co. Ltd. is located in the grasslands in Xingjian Autonomous Region, one of the three largest pastures in China. It enjoys great geographic advantage and unique natural conditions. Shihezi City, where the company is headquartered, is at the center of the North-Piedmont Economic Zone of the Tianshan Mountains in Xinjiang. As a high quality milk source, it attracted many famous domestic dairy product companies such as YiLi, Wahaha, Wangwang to make investment and set up plants in Shihezi. All this investment enabled Shihezi to become one of the most important milk bases in China.

The full name of the Western Husbandry is Western Animal Husbandry Co., Ltd., which was jointly founded by the Xinjiang TianRong Investment (Group) Co., Ltd. and Western Xinjiang Public (Group) Co., Ltd. in June 18, 2003, with registered capital RMB 6.6 million. Xinjiang TianRong Investment (Group) invested RMB 6.1 million in cash, which accounts for 92.42 % of the total registered capital. The Western Xinjiang Public (Group) invested RMB 0.5 million in cash, which accounts for about 7.58 % of the registered capital.[6]

The three primary subsidiaries of the Western are engaged in company's different businesses, respectively. Among them, Quansheng Animal Husbandry is specialized in the feedstock. As the base for the feedstock processing, Quansheng provides high quality feedstock to the parent company and other individual farmers who have joined Western's professional services system. Depending upon its years of experience and continuous improvement on ingredients, Quansheng plays a significant role in increasing the attractiveness of its parent company's professional service system to the small individual farmers, and its high quality feedstock has greatly improved the yield of the cows.

Tianyuan Milk Co., Ltd. mainly focused on the purchasing and sales of raw milk before 2009. Since then, it has shifted its focus towards the production and sales of feedstock. Manas Farm, the third subsidiary, is primarily engaged in the breeding of dairy cattle, which is a part of the core of the primary business of its

6 All data of Western Animal Husbandry used in this chapter are from Initial Public Offering Prospectus of Western Animal Husbandry unless indicated otherwise.

parent company. It was founded for meeting the increasing demand of the downstream dairy processing companies, expanding the scale of raw milk production and raising the sales revenue. It is worth mentioning that Aorixin Biotechnology, another subsidiary of Western, provides main technical support to its parent company, including embryo sexing and elite breeding.

Western was listed in Shenzhen Stock Exchange in August 20, 2010 (Stock Ticker: 300106), raising 357 million RMB with issuing of 30 million outstanding shares. The issuing price was RMB 11.90 per share and PE ratio was 51.74 (diluted).

## 4.3 Parallel Development Strategies

There are three main business lines for Western Animal Husbandry: sales of the raw milk collected from outside farms, sales of self-produced raw milk and elite breeding. Among them, there are some overlapping of the sales of the raw milk collected from outside farms and elite breeding. Meanwhile, the sales of the raw milk collected from outside farms and the sales of self-produced raw milk can also be collectively categorized as the sales of raw milk.

The uniqueness of the Western's business model lies on its creative parallel-development strategy of build-up of large scaled farms and standardization of milk producing procedures with many scattered smaller sized farms, which represents a decentralized scaled-production. Under this model, Western can raise the cow in its own large scaled farms. Meanwhile, the raw milk is collected from both the cattle farms of the company itself and the co-ups with other individual farmers to guarantee the adequate supply.

The firms in the upstream of the milk industry are exposed with much higher risks comparing with downstream firms, and with less profit as well. From the experience of many developed countries, it's pretty obvious that large-scaled breeding is the best way out. Take U.S. for example, the dairy farms are mainly owned and managed by individual families which is similar to China's case. However, the raw milk production in the U.S. is highly centralized. The number of small dairy farms with less than 30 cows merely accounts for 30 % of all the dairy farms and the raw milk production from the small farms only takes for about 1 % of the entire productions.[7] As a matter of fact, the raw milk in the US market is primarily provided by a few large dairy farms. The benefits of the large scaled breeding are many, including that better cow species can be cultivated and epidemics can be better prevented. More importantly, the raw milk yield can be adjusted according to the actual market demand to reduce the inventory cost. This model is apparently meaningful for the future development for the milk industry in China.

---

[7] ChangJiang Security: http://www.95579.com/, also, Initial Public Offering Prospectus of Western Animal Husbandry.

Western, as a pioneer, actually took this path of large scaled breeding. Currently, the company already owns six large-scaled farms with modern cattle sheds and production equipment which are the most advanced facilities in Xinjiang Autonomous Region, and elite cultivars were also imported from Australia.

However, immediately starting build-up of large scaled breeding farm in a wide scope may not be possible due to a number of reasons. First, large scale breeding requires not only big capital investment but also many natural or geographic conditions. For example, large scale breeding requires flat, dry, leeward and tranquil land, with smooth drainage and exposure to the sun. It also requires sufficient water resources and good quality grassland. What's more, technical professionals are essential for wastewater treatment and manure disposal. So it's difficult to establish many such large-scale dairy farms in a short period of time in China due to the shortage of these resources, in particular, the capital and professionals.

On the other hand, the market demand for fresh milk is far more than the possible supply that can be produced by only a few large scaled farms. The demand for fresh milk is high because of the large population and increased average daily intake in China in the recent years. Currently, the massive market demand for milk is mainly supplied by the many smaller sized individual dairy farmers. However, because of the insufficient capital investment and lack of the needed technology improvement, it is impractical to simply drop these individual farmers or to merge them into some large scaled breeding farms. Meanwhile, it would go back to the old fashion if just letting some companies or milk stations simply to collect the raw milk from these small milk farmers, then, sell the collected milk to the downstream processing companies. As mentioned earlier, this old-fashion model can neither provide a decent profit margin for the small individual farmers, as they are in a buyer's market, nor guarantee the quality of milk collected from small farmers. As a result, an alternative model that processing company which collects milk from small farms also provides cultivation technology and support to the individual farmers to standardize the production process and enhance the quality of milk seems the direction to go. With the support of government policies, this is the way that Western Animal Husbandry actually took, and is proved a win–win strategy for both Western and small milk farms.

## 4.4 The Parallel Model: Western's Competitive Advantage

Western Animal Husbandry provides many services to the individual farmers, including elite breeding, cultivation techniques, disease prevention and control, milking facilities, cold chain transportation, and also conducts source control, process control and quality control. As long as the milk meets the quality standard of Western, the company would collect all the raw milk from the suppliers and take care of the cold chain transportation and milk sales. These services are major parts of the primary businesses of Western Animal Husbandry. In particular, elite breeding plays a critical role in large scale breeding because only fine breeds can increase milk yields. However, investment in the elite breeding would increase the unit cost of fresh milk if the fine breed is not a stand-alone business, instead, is only a byproduct of scaled breeding and milk production. Therefore, running elite breeding as a stand-alone primary business will lower the unit cost of self-produced milk production.

On the profit side, as an upstream company in the supply chain, Western Animal Husbandry sells raw milk to the downstream processing companies. The sales of raw milk collected by Western from the individual farmers counts for about 71.88 % of the total revenue of the milk sold, which is pretty much consistent with the whole current market structure that the milk production from the small individual farmers make up for 60 % of the total milk output. As a consequence, more individual farmers sign contracts with the Western, the more monopoly power the Western would gain, and Western would be in a better position in the negotiation with the downstream companies, and control of the profit distribution in the value chain.

## 4.5 The Parallel Model: Gains for Small Suppliers

With the breeding technique support and the uniformed milking and cold transportation provided from the milk companies such as Western, the farmer can not only increase the milk yield but also better prevent epidemics and diseases. At the result, the quality of raw milk is improved and the use of toxic chemicals such as the melamine can be better prevented. Meanwhile, as a small farm without strong bargaining power, signing long term contract with Western can help reduce the potential loss from the variation of milk price and market demand.

In addition, as a supplementary business, Western also provides feedstock services for small dairy farmer with some specialized feedstock recipe, such as clove, ensiling, pasture harvesting, and tractor-plough. As a matter of fact, there is great demand for such services in the neighboring regions of the Western Animal Husbandry. As stated in a local government planning document titled "Development Program of High Quality Cows in Shihezi Prefecture", there will be 15 super large high-quality milk production centers with more than 60,000 cows and more than 1,000 large scale individual farmers,[8] and more than 2,500 small-scaled individual farmers[9] located in that area in the near future; and the small individual farmers will be managing totally around 50,000 cows. The milk yield of the cow will reach about 5,000 kg per cow, and thus the total milk yield is about 0.2 million ton per annum which could provide sufficient milk for the processing

---

[8] A large scale individual farmer is defined as a farmer with more than 10 cows individually.

[9] A small scale individual farmer refers to the farmer with two cows on average each.

companies. And all these individual farmers are exactly the target customers of the Western's supplementary business.

Therefore, the supply of raw milk is the core business of the Western Animal Husbandry. The elite breeding, feedstock, pasture harvesting, and the tractor-plough are the supporting lines. Western Animal Husbandry well integrated all these business lines. On one hand, Western successfully consolidated the raw milk sources by providing a one-stop shopping supplementary services for many small milk farmers and made them part of Western's milk supply system; on the other hand, this consolidation enabled Western to provide sufficient high-quality milk to the end dairy consumers, and helped Western gain a significant share in the marketplace.

## 4.6 Winning Through Technology

Another distinct feature in Western's business model is its long-term collaboration with academic institutions and universities on the R&D. Western jointly established several research centers with universities, and periodically invited both domestic and international experts to the company for consulting and information sharing that kept the company up to the most updated technology innovation and their future development trend.

As a result, Western gained significant technology advantage comparing with its competitors. The milk yield of cows in Xinjiang is, on average, about 2–5 tons per annum; while the imported or improved varieties cultivated by the Western can produce a yield of about 7–8 tons per annum, which brought great economic benefits for Western Animal Husbandry.

## 4.7 The Extended Supply Chain

On the downstream, Western Animal Husbandry also set up some long-term and stable relationships with many famous dairy product companies such as Yili, Wangwang, Wahaha, Maiquer, and Huayuan through joint ventures or supply agreements. Higher quality raw milk is in great demand with higher price. In order to receive high quality milk these downstream companies all set up their manufacturing plants in Xinjiang that provide Western a great opportunity to collaborate with these downstream firms in a close way. This cooperation guarantees the market for Western's raw milk and reduces risk on sales. At the same time, as the source of the raw milk, Western's collaboration with the downstream companies also provided the Western a near-monopolistic power in price bargaining and deal negotiation.

## 4.8 A Small Company with Large Market Share

Western's decentralized standardization model also helped the firm to be able to compete with its larger competitors. In several key markets of Xinjiang, the major competitor of Western is Xinjiang Hutubi Breeding Cattle Farm, a large stated-owned enterprise. As a red hat (state owned) company, Hutubi has strong policy support from government and also possessed some technology advantages. Hutubi's main business is the cattle breeding and cow raise, but with multiple other business lines such as agriculture, milk products processing, embryo transfer and feedstock production. However, comparing with Western, there is no scattered breeding in Hutubi, and they have to heavily rely on their own large pasture and hiring of local farmers. Such business model can provide the firm some decent gross profit margin but not in a large quantity, at least in the near future. As a result, Western Animal Husbandry, even though it is not the largest milk farm in terms of the number of cows it owned directly, controls more than 80 % of the raw milk supply in Xinjiang and enjoys a near-monopsony power.

## 4.9 Decentralized Standardization and Centralized in House Production

The average milk consumption level in China, as mentioned earlier, is relatively lower than the international level, indicating there is a great potential for the future growth. For example, the school milk program alone would generate tremendous demand for milk. In China, there are over 200 million elementary, middle and high school students, and it is expected that more than 25 million students will drink milk at school by 2015,[10] which is equivalent to the consumption of about 2 million tons of milk per year. In addition, the China's ambitious urbanization plan will also increase the demand for milk. For each new comer of the city, the demand for milk will be increased by 5 kg per person per year. Such solid growing demand provided great growth opportunity for the companies in the dairy industry.

To seize such opportunity, Western also adopted a double-play strategy. On one hand, the company built up large-scaled farm to breed more cows in house that increased milk yield by breeding variety cows, and improved milk quality by better control of the production process. On the other hand, the company also increased the purchase of raw milk from the external individual farmers, by adopting these scattered small farmer into Western's standardized system, and providing various professional services such as elite breeding, cultivation techniques, disease prevention and control, milking facilities, cold chain transportation, source control, process control and quality control to standardize the

[10] Founder Security, 'New Leader of the Milk Industry', http://www.foundersc.com/

production process of external companies as well. As a result, it created virtuous cycle that further brings Western continuous growth and profitability as indicated by the company's data in the past and future projection.

The raw milk sales in 2009, in terms of volume, were 8,132 tons, with an increase of 31.73 % over 2008. And the raw milk sales in 2008 were 6,173 tons, with an increase of 16.41 % over 2007. The primary reason for such growth was attributed to the development of large scaled breeding that helps the company to improve the quality of its milk and gain the recognition for its better milk in the market. On the external purchasing side, the sales volume of externally purchased milk in 2009 was 82,990 tons, going up by 6.40 % than that of 2008. The sales volume of externally purchased milk in 2008 was 78,001 tons, going up by 16.97 % than the year before. The main reason for the growth was attributed to the continued improvement of professional services Western provided to the external farmers. These enhanced services attracted more farmers to sign contracts with Western to join Western's decentralized standardization process to provide milk that meets Western's standard. On the financial side, according to the forecasts generated by security companies,[11] the sales revenue increased to RMB 655 million in 2012, a rise of 145 % than the RMB 267 million in 2009.

Moving along with the increase in sales, the gross margin also increased significantly and contributed to the fast growth of overall profit. The increase of gross margin was actually achieved through a decrease of cost per unit which is the direct result of the economy of scale and Western's effort on building up of its own large scaled farms. In addition, the improvement in management system and the application of new technologies also played important roles. For examples, the importing of higher yield dairy cow can definitely increase the total output with the same cost per unit, and the embryo technology can improve the cow varieties and the milk quality. A typical example is the imported Holstein dairy cow, whose yield is about 8 tons per annum, which is much higher than the average level of the domestic cows in the market. The sales of these imported cows by Western to external farmers have significantly improved the productivity of the external smaller farmers. The sales revenue from this part of Western business has reached RMB 14 million, and still keeps growing.

## 4.10 Expansion through Vertical Integration

In addition to its core businesses, Western Animal Husbandry has been actively extending its business lines by developing beef cattle and breeding cattle. The company currently has more than 400 Red Angus breeding cattle with top meat quality, and well positioned itself in the high end beef market. Geographically, Western's expansion was not limited only in the Xinjiang market but also

[11] Founder Security, 'New Leader of the Milk Industry', http://www.foundersc.com/

expanding to other parts of China by joining in the National Cattle Reserve Program.

Western Animal Husbandry also acquired the Garden Milk Product Company with the intention to integrate the entire industry value chain. Western bought 60 % of the Garden Milk Product Company's equity by RMB 8.4 million, entering into the raw milk processing market and gained control of the entire supply chain, and covering feedstock production, cow breeding, raw milk collection, milk processing, the intermediate products, and the final end dairy products. As stated by Western's Board Chairman, the merger of the Western Animal Husbandry and the Garden Milk Product is not only a perfect combination of resources, capital and brand, but also an important step for the Western Animal Husbandry to enter into the milk processing business. After the merger and acquisition, The Garden Milk Product Company will continue its traditional business on the high value-added infant milk formula and other milk products. Meanwhile, Western Animal Husbandry will continue to integrate the milk industry value chain, first in the neighboring pastures in Shihezi City area. In the near future, with its high quality products and geographic advantages, Western Animal Husbandry can easily enter into the markets of bigger cities such as Urumqi and Kuytun. Western's integration strategy helped better balance the profit distribution among different business lines to avoid profits being skewed towards only the downstream lines, and generated more growth spots for the company. At the end, Western is moving towards a comprehensive company with multiple lines covering dairy products, beef cattle, and breeding cattle.

## 4.11 Moving Towards Modern Agriculture

With the funds raised from the capital market, Western Animal Husbandry established a standardized breeding base with 6,000 high-yield cattle and a technology research center focused on varieties breeding. This standardized breeding base alone can generate enormous profits for the firm through increased milk yield, delicacy management, reduced breeding cost, the economy of scale, and technical support on environmental protection, biogas utilization, ensiling feedstock seed and other areas. Given the constantly increased domestic demand, the self-produced raw milk can create much higher gross profit margin. The larger the proportions of self-produced milk in the total sales of raw milk, the greater the company's profit.

At the same time, large-scaled breeding is a trend for the development of the modern new agriculture. It can alleviate land desertification and receive more favorable policies from government. The effort on the large-scaled breeding significantly helped the company to become the role model of the industry and promote Western's brand. But, meanwhile, Western Animal Husbandry didn't overlook the way to collect the raw milk from outside farmers. As a matter of fact, the company continued to enhance its "decentralized-scaled-standardization" model by making additional investment on building 40 large milking halls and purchasing constant-temperature vehicles for the milk collected from outside farmers. This double-play strategy continued to strengthen western's leading position in the dairy industry for the years to come.

# Chapter 5
# The King of Mobile Game: The Story of Ourpalm

**Abstract** This chapter discusses the case of Ourpalm, a leading mobile game developer in China's emerging gaming industry. As a fast growing market with intricate players, the gaming industry has made it difficult for many companies to gain a competitive advantage. Ourpalm developed a successful business model that made it stand out from its many competitors by becoming an integrator of the industry value chain.

**Keywords** Mobile game · PC game · TV game · Online game · Mobile network game platform

Young fans of mobile games may not have heard of Ourpalm, a mobile game company from China, but they almost definitely have heard of Spongebob Squarepants, or 24 h. Ourpalm is the official authorized developer of the Chinese version of these two popular games, and is also the partner of big names in the gaming industry such as Digital Chocolate and EA. As the second online game company to be listed in China's Shenzhen A-share stock market (Ticker: 300315), Ourpalm's major investors include Huayi Brothers, a famous movie maker, who is Ourpalm's second largest shareholder. Looking at the Shenzhen Stock Exchange's records on the day of Ourpalm's IPO, Ourpalm's initial fund-raising target was RMB 200 million, but it turned out to raise over RMB 650 million. During the preliminary inquiry period, there were 76 share-allotment participants represented by 45 inquiry agents who were involved in the offering, and the ratio of institutional subscription was as high as 11.38 times.[1] Let's take a look at what they did and what happened in China's complex mobile game industry in the following sections.

---

[1] China Times: http://stock.hexun.com/2012-05-12/141336845.html

J. G. Wang and J. Yang, *Who Gets Funds from China's Capital Market?*,
SpringerBriefs in Business, DOI: 10.1007/978-3-642-44913-0_5, 

## 5.1 The Mobile Space

In this day and age, "mobile games" signifies something much more than a game that simply "moves". Mobile games are games that can be played using mobile handheld devices such as a mobile phone or tablet. The electronic game industry that is often talked about can actually be divided into several more specific categories, as shown in the following chart.

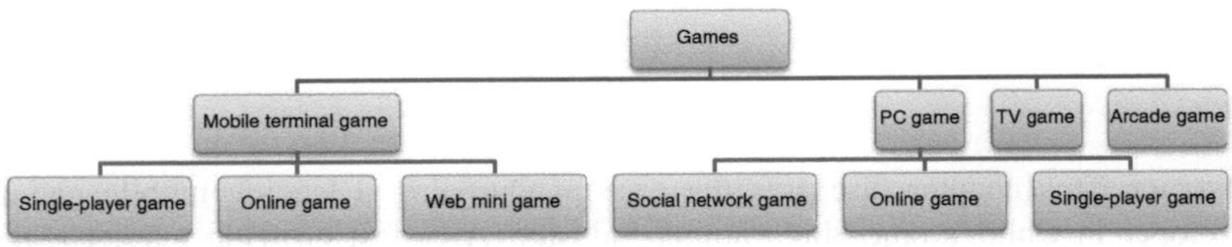


Where do mobile games fit in? In fact, they belong to the first layer category from the left, the mobile terminal games. The reason for why all terminals are lumped together is because terminals such as mobile phones or tablet PCs are only of small difference to the game developers. Disney, for example, would not discard the iPad version of the "Where Is My Water" game just because its iPhone version of it turned out to be so successful; and vice versa, once the game became successful on one terminal, Disney would be sure to transition it to others.

The umbrella term mobile terminal game is reserved for the games running on all mobile terminals. In China, these are still mainly phone-based. In general, mobile terminal games consist of single-player games, online games, mini-web games, among others. Single-player games refer to games that run on a mobile phone with or without a mobile network connection in order to activate service, process payment, or upload game credits. Mini-web games refer to games that users can play on WAP pages directly, without using customer end programs. Online games refer to games which require users to play on the customer end program as well as interact with other players through the mobile network and game server, excluding those which solely need a mobile network to achieve activation or upload game credits.

Before 2010, the business of Ourpalm pretty much focused on single-player games and mini-web games within the mobile terminal category. With the continuous integration of the Internet and mobile network, as well as the increased market demand for cross-platform game products, Ourpalm began to engage in the development and operation of social network games in 2010. Using its competitive advantage and business experience, it then entered into the sector of cross-platform games.

## 5.2 Players in the Space

The value chain of the mobile game industry, as presented in the chart below, consists of primarily the game publisher, game developer, service provider, mobile carrier, mobile phone manufacturers and end users. The participation of all parties in the chain is necessary for this industry function properly.

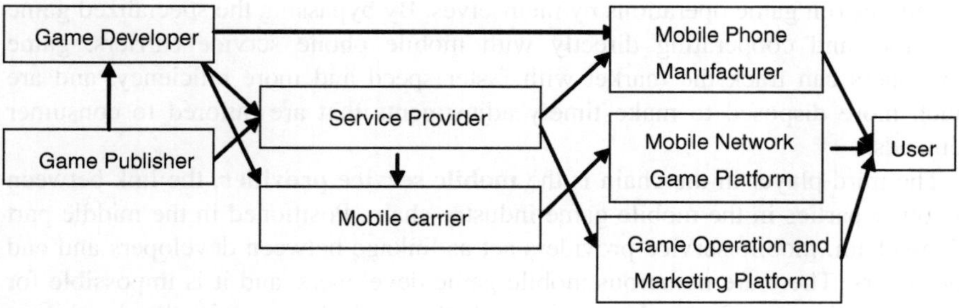


The first participant in the value chain is the **game publisher**, the provider for the game content. The game publisher sits on the upstream end of the supply chain. Since mobile games have only recently been introduced in China, this segment of the market is far from mature. Primarily, disputes of copyright tend to occur from time to time as copyrights are oftentimes unclear and there exists unauthorized development without license due to the nascent nature of the Chinese mobile game publishing industry.

The second player in the value chain is the **game developer**, essentially the producer of the games. Game developers have the functionality and ability to transform the content of mobile games into a sellable product, and hence, are the pivotal cogs in the industry. However, as the threshold for being a developer is relatively low, there exist many mobile game developers, both large and small. This leads to fierce competition, with the result of competition being a mixed blessing for the companies involved. On one hand, developers in China's market with real competitive advantages such as Ourpalm can successfully withstand the harsh competitive environment because of their high quality products that have already been recognized by the market. On the other hand, developers of lesser quality products may end up fishing in troubled waters, turning to plagiarizing other developers' products to maintain their bottom lines. The prevalence of plagiarizing not only results in losses to high-quality mobile game developers, but also leads to homogeneity of products in the mobile gaming market, which is detrimental to the industry's development as a whole.

Since game developers are at the lower end of the value chain, their main task is to develop new games. Then, through the service provider, these games will enter the channels of mobile service providers where end consumers can download them to their mobile phones via their networks. Other alternatives are that the mobile game developers can collaborate directly with mobile service carriers, or they can build their own operating platform. As developers are not in direct contact with the end consumers, feedbacks from the end users can only be obtained through game operators and/or mobile phone service carriers. This results in an inevitable time lag for these feedbacks to reach the developers, which is also detrimental to developers in tracking and providing quality service to their audience.

In order to mitigate the intermediary effect, some game developers with stronger operating capacities, such as Kongzhong.com, MIG, and Ourpalm, sometimes run game operations by themselves. By bypassing the specialized game operators and cooperating directly with mobile phone service carriers, game developers can track the market with faster speed and more efficiency, and are much more disposed to make timely adjustments that are tailored to consumer demands.

The third player in the chain is the **mobile service provider**, the link between the other parties in the mobile game industry chain. Positioned in the middle part of the chain, mobile service providers act as linkage between developers and end consumers. There are numerous mobile game developers, and it is impossible for mobile carriers to effectively engage with them all. As a result, the developers usually just commission or sell products directly to game service providers, and simply delegate them the task of actually providing the games to end players. Some relatively large domestic mobile phone operators include SNDA Digital-Red, Sina Mobile Games, Kongzhong.com, Linktone, MIG, Pear in Palm, to just name a few.

As the industry of mobile games gradually matures, however, game developers may also grow to a point where they can bypass game service providers and cooperate with mobile carriers directly. Faced with this imminent threat, many game service providers are now trying to obtain qualifications for game development by acquiring shares, pursuing mergers/acquisitions with mobile game developers, or becoming a two-in-one, a company as both game developer and service provider.

The fourth player is the **mobile phone manufacturer**, the carrier of the mobile phone game industry chain. Mobile phone manufacturers act as the provider of mobile game carrier in the mobile game industry chain. In reality, mobile games and PC games are quite different, as there is a compatibility issue for mobile games that exists only on a small scale for PC games. The same mobile game might not be able to be played on different mobile phones with different brands, or even sometimes on different models of the same brand. Thus, game developers need to develop different versions of same games according to different phone brands and models, which significantly increase the cost of mobile game development.

On the other side, for phone companies, there is a certain gap between the maneuverability, visual presentation and intelligence of mobile phone games versus the same games on PC. For the most part, the PC is still superior in delivering on all three aspects. As a result, many mobile phone manufacturers have introduced smart phones with large, high-resolution touch screen in order to improve consumers' satisfaction when it comes to mobile games.

The next player in the industry is the **mobile phone service carrier**, the channel provider in the chain. Compared to the other participants, mobile service carriers have almost absolute power in the mobile game industry chain. Its relationship with game operators and game developers is very much like the relationship between a supervisor and his supervisee. With their purveyance over the mobile network, billing channels, and mobile games application platforms such as the SMS platform, the JAVA platform, and the BREW platform, they hold the reins in the industry. As a hot spot for mobile data services, mobile games have attracted widespread attention from various carriers—they realized that taking advantage of mobile games and focusing on their development could bring significant boosts to average revenue per user (ARPU).

Currently, the mobile game platforms offered by mobile phone service carriers are far from convenient for the majority of game players to download. As a result, for the time being, platforms offered by mobile game service providers instead of mobile carriers still widely appear on the market, allowing users to achieve more convenient game downloading.

However, mobile carriers are not satisfied to simply act as a download channel for mobile phone games. By actively developing their own games and setting up their own operation teams, mobile carriers decided to compete head-to-head with mobile game developers and service providers using their network advantages. In 2009, China Mobile built a mobile game production base in Jiangsu Province in order to enhance their capabilities in mobile game development and services. China Unicom also began building value-added service bases, now up to six of them, including a mobile game base. In addition, the development of the 3G network laid the foundation for mobile online games which can be played at greatly enhanced speeds.

The final cog in the industry machine is the **mobile game player**, the end consumers in mobile game industry chain. The ultimate purpose of all the preceding development is to meet the needs of end users. Demographically, mobile game consumers can currently be described by a "three-low" set of characteristics—that is, low income, low age, and low level of education. On the gender side, male mobile game players account for 92.8 % of total players, clearly much higher proportionally than females. This signals huge development potential for the mobile game market. Even just looking at gender, mobile game developers have the potential to develop more games in accordance with the preferences of female game players to capture that completely untapped market. In addition, the industry can also develop games tailored to the preferences of different ages, so as to improve its penetration in different age groups.

To sum up the value chain discussion, the mobile game industry in China is already in place, but, as a newly developed industry, there are certainly many issues that need to be resolved within the many parts of the value chain. Meanwhile, the nascent industry is providing fast growing companies such as Ourpalm with an enormously large platform on which to work, and a huge audience to capture.

## 5.3 What They Hold in Their Palm

Started in the Zhongguancun Science and Technology Park in Beijing's Silicon Valley, Ourpalm Co., Ltd. was set up in August 2004 with a registered capital of RMB 164 million. As a high-tech firm with certificates for both software products and software enterprises, Ourplam specialized in game development, issuance, and operations. As a result of its reputation as a leading mobile game developer, issuer, and operator in China, Ourpalm successfully listed on the Shenzhen Stock Exchange on May 11th, 2012. The main scope of its businesses includes development, distribution, promotion, operation and maintenance of mobile games, internet games and other related products. Ourpalm currently has more than 400 employees, and more than 190 product lines of games have been developed. Its revenue in 2011 increased by 56.55 % over the previous year.[2]

### *5.3.1 Who Owns Ourplam?*

Prior to IPO, Wenbin Yao, Chairman of the Board, and Yingtao Ye, Director and General Manager, jointly held 61,074,000 shares of the company, which accounted for 49.76 % of the total shares before the company got listed. As persons-acting-in-concert as stated in an agreement, the two of them are joint-owners of the firm and share control accordingly.

Next after Yao and Ye, the third most notable shareholder of the firm following the public listing is Huayi Brothers, a well-known filmmaker in China. Through acquisition and its subsequent capital injection of total RMB 148.5 million in June 2010, Huayi Brothers obtained 22 % of Ourpalm's shares, and signed an agreement with Ourplam which stated that upon becoming the second largest shareholder of Ourpalm, Huayi Brothers would offer its movie and TV products to Ourpalm for the latter to develop corresponding mobile games, web games and social network games. Essentially, Ourpalm obtained priority in getting authorization to produce the games based on Huayi's movie and TV products.[3] Only five months after the signing of the agreement, Ourpalm got the game development authorization for three popular Huayi Brothers' movies, and quickly introduced the games to market. Development of mobile games basing on TV series was in line with the game development trend of the time, and allowed Ourpalm to significantly avoid homogeneous competition. Ourpalm also took advantage of the marketing resources of TV stations to promote the development of their mobile game business.

[2] Sina Finance: http://vip.stock.finance.sina.com.cn/corp/go.php/vFD_FinanceSummary/stockid/300315.phtml#2011-12-31

[3] Tencent: http://tech.qq.com/a/20120327/000230.htm

This is only a part of the story—what else was it that made investors so optimistic about Ourpalm? Let's take a closer look at Ourpalm's core competencies in its production, promotion, and integration of the industry value chain.

### 5.3.2 The Linchpin of Success: Competitive R&D

As previously discussed, game development in China is still far behind that of Europe and the United States, and, as a part of that industry, Ourpalm is not an exception. However, compared to its domestic counterparts, Ourpalm have some distinct advantages, thanks to its strategic approaches and capabilities. One of these advantages is in its game development capability. By the time the mobile gaming industry had begun to flourish in China, Ourpalm's game products had already gained certain brand recognition in the market place. Ourpalm closely tracked the technological development of smart phone platforms such as Android and iOS in order to gain a leading position in the smart phone game market, and subsequently developed the capability for game development based on these "smart" platforms. So far, Ourpalm has launched several games based on such platforms, such as "Hot-blooded Genghis Khan Online," a mobile network game which was based on the Android and J2ME, and the single-player game "Colorful Bubble," which was iOS based and ranked 1st in the free game category on the App Store in early October of 2011.

The game products that were independently developed by Ourpalm were already covered wide areas of the game industry including mobile terminal games, social network games, and cross-platform games. Ourpalm also possessed multiple types of game development engines and large-scaled game development teams. One such development engine was the On-Air-Cross-Platform Online Game Development Engine, which was created by Ourpalm's subsidiary Dalian Wolong and supported PC Web browser along with a bunch of terminal platform such as the J2ME, Symbian, the iPhone, MTK, and WinCE. Ourpalms even possessed a game simulation engine which was developed independently by its subsidiary FMworlds.

### 5.3.3 The Shade of a Big Tree

Ourplam fully understood that mobile carriers held the tremendous power in the mobile game industry. Since the very beginning, it cleverly developed and maintained a strong, trusting relationship with China Mobile, China's largest mobile carrier. Among all of China Mobile's business partners, Ourpalm ranked top three, and had been named many times an "outstanding game business partner" of China Mobile. Ourpalm's partnership has brought it great bounties—as a result of the connection, Ourpalm is now able to issue hundreds of single-player games through China Mobile's game portal, including four game packages in China Mobile's G + platform, and it has also earned display spots on the game portal of China Mobile's Monternet. Ourpalm's settlement revenue from China Mobile accounted for 61.15, 56.56 and 65.39 % of its total operating income from 2009 to 2011, respectively.[4]

### 5.3.4 *Not All Eggs in One Basket*

Ourplam is one of the companies in the gaming industry that truly understood the concept of diversification of risk, and didn't put all their eggs in one basket. Simultaneous to maintaining its relationship with China Mobile, Ourpalm also developed close collaborations with other major Internet portals: WAP sites, professional gaming sites, mobile device manufacturers and application platform developers. Since February 2007, Ourpalm has established long-term cooperative relationships with UCWeb, 3G Portal, Kongzhong.com, d.cn, Tencent, joyes.com, and mobile phone manufacturers such as Nokia, Motorola, Sony Ericsson, and Samsung for mobile portal access and game pre-installment. On December 2009, Ourpalm worked with the iPhone app store on online games, and with Sky-mobi for broad channel promotion.[5] Meanwhile, Ourpalm is also constantly consolidating and strengthening its own gaming platform such as the "Gamebean" and "Union.Gamebean" platform, which have become major domestic mobile games issuance platforms. "Union.Gamebean" was the first marketing platform for licensed mobile games, and it has cooperated with hundreds of Internet, WAP, and mobile phone manufacturers to promote its mobile games, successfully organizing a number of mobile games themed activities which allowed Ourpalm to gain higher visibility with end consumers.

### 5.3.5 *Vertical Integration: First-Mover Advantage*

In a competitive market like the mobile gaming industry, integrating the industry value chain through strategic partnerships or mergers and acquisitions is known to effectively generate synergy and offer competitive advantages. In this regard, Ourpalm set a great example.

Naturally, the quality of licensed mobile games depends directly upon the quality of the resources on which they are based, such as movies, TV series or other licensed products. Maintaining a close relationship with film and TV products makers is thus critical for mobile game providers to be successful. By getting

[4] Prospectus of Ourpalm Co.,Ltd.

[5] Economic Information: http://jjckb.xinhuanet.com/invest/2012-05/11/content_374719.htm

Huayi Brothers, one of the most influential movie makers in China, as its second largest shareholder, Ourplam gained a huge advantage in its development of high quality games based on high-quality movie and TV products.

On another front, Ourpalm also acquired three game developers with strong technical backgrounds since September 2009—G9, Dalian Wolong and FMworld—to enrich its independent research and development capacity. G9 had rich experience in action puzzle-related single-player mobile games. Dalian Wolong was experienced in single-player game transfers, MTK platform game development, and it possessed key technologies in cross-platform game development engines. Finally, FMworld had profound technical strength in the areas of sports simulation development, and owned key technologies for game simulation engines.

At the current stage of the China's mobile game market development, the main players are positioned in a relatively dispersed manner. As can be expected, the ultimate industry leader will be bound to a small number of companies that have strong integration capabilities, and these firms are the ones that will gain tremendous first-mover advantage. The reason is very simple.

Companies always want to occupy the most valuable, most lucrative spot in the industrial value chain. However, that spot tends to be reserved for very few companies, and it is impossible for all sectors to become the most valuable. That is why extending and integrating a company along its industrial chain tends to mean higher operating efficiency, greater profit margin and more favorable market positioning, since all companies will be able to integrate quality resources through mergers and acquisitions. Seeing as high-quality resources are so limited in the industry, late-comers take the risk of coming up empty-handed when they do their target search.

Consequently, the synergy in any kind of integration can only be perfected over time, and the time needed for an effective system integration following an M&A is no exception. Any M&A transaction is succeeded by a period of personnel reshuffling, adoption of different corporate cultures and management styles, and numerous other logistical issues. It is because of this that it is difficult for late-comers to develop any kind of competitive advantage in a short period of time in this industry. Early-comers such as Ourpalm, on the other hand, possess tremendous and irreproducible competitive advantage in the marketplace. As a result of all these forces, it can be expected that the mobile game industry will witness a new development trend where the "strong" will become stronger, and the degree of the concentration in market will be significantly increased.

## 5.4 Money in the Palm of Our Hands

Ourpalm managed to make a successful listing in Shenzhen Stock Exchange in 2005, almost undoubtedly because its successful business model convinced investors to hand over capital to Ourpalm's—well, palms. Digging a little deeper, we can understand why investors were so optimistic about Ourpalm.

At the industry level, with the popularity of mobile phones, tablet PCs and other mobile terminals, and also with the growth of mobile networks, the number of mobile phone users continues to rise. And as the mobile apps market gets more and more mature, the mobile network market is experiencing rapid revenue growth. According to a forecast by Analysys, the scale of China's mobile network market will reach 320.4 billion by the end of 2013 with a 61.9 % compounding annual growth rate from 2011 to 2013. Users will reach 749 million with a 31.8 % compounding annual growth rate from 2011 to 2013.[6] Such a huge user base has laid a solid foundation for the rapid growth of the mobile games market, and this forecast is certainly not lost on equity investors.

There are, however, so many players in this market—game developers, mobile phone service carriers, mobile game service providers, other subsidiary parties. With limited funds available from investors, which sector is most likely to become the king of mobile games in the near future?

Though this is just a prediction, it seems quite clear that game developers have the largest amount of potential, for several reasons. First, the future development of the mobile games industry seems that it will place the most importance on developers. Compared single-player games, mobile terminal network games are becoming increasingly more popular with end consumers thanks to their "anytime, anywhere" characteristic. In fact, the latter's share in total market revenue has increased year by year for the last half decade. Online games, including mobile games, generate profits primarily through value-added services, such as the purchase of props or charges for locked areas. The final product, therefore, needs to organize a series of activities, such as game competition, to provide value-added services to end users. This process cannot be undertaken only by the promotional platforms at the lower end of the industry value chain, because they typically do not fully understand the background of game operations. It is the developers that possess detailed data about user behavior and fully understand the intricacies of game development, and, as a result, are in a much better position to integrate the value chain. For the most part, developers do this by expanding further to the downstream part of operations.

Second, when Apple's content-based-sales model succeeded, many game service providers and mobile carriers tried to emulate Apple, indicating that at the very least, the software application shopping mall in the near future will become a rather hilarious and lively place. As future promotion channels for games become more diversified, competition between the channels will intensify as well. To attract more users, mobile phone companies will have to depend much more heavily on game developers, causing these developers to take a stronger position in the market.

Needless to say, innovation and quality are the soul of development in the mobile games industry, and the most critical factor in attracting end users. It is the game developers that bear the responsibility to continuously conduct innovation

6 Analysys International: http://english.analysys.com.cn/

and enhance the content of their games. As of present, the mobile game industry in China is still characterized by a large numbers of mobile game suppliers, a generally low quality of content, a lack of innovation, and serious homogenization. The market in the next few years is bound to face increased competition and constant reshuffling. Under such a market environment, it is not a surprise at all that Ourpalm successfully distinguished itself from its peers through its continuously enhanced game development capability, wide distribution channels, and excellent integration capability of the industry value chain. It has truly become a star in China's equity market.

# Chapter 6
# You Only Need to Dial One Number: The Story About Eternal Asia

**Abstract** As outsourcing of non-core businesses steadily becomes a global trend, companies who provide outsourcing services have begun to flourish. Started as a logistics service provider for Cisco, Eternal Asia, the company that will be discussed in this chapter, quickly refined and perfected the concept of supply chain management and capitalized on these global trends. On top of this, it went a step further to develop a supply chain financing model that provides significant value for the financing of SMEs in general.

**Keywords** Logistics market · Outsourcing of non-core business · Supply chain management · E-commerce · Supply chain financing · One-stop-shopping

Eternal Asia? It's another name you probably never heard before, but, in fact, it is the logistic service provider for Cisco, General Electric, AMD, Philips, and a whole bunch of other Fortune 500 companies—companies that you definitely have heard of. Established in 1997, it is located in Shenzhen, China, under the official name Eternal Asia Supply Chain Management Ltd. It currently operates with 9 branches, 18 subsidiaries, and employs over 3,000 people around the world.

Eternal Asia is a fast growing company. In late 2007, Eternal Asia successfully listed in the Shenzhen Stock Exchange (Ticker: 002183), with the first-day stock trading price up over 111 % from the opening one. By 2011, its sales reached RMB 34.5 billion with an operating income of RMB 7 billion, and a net profit 130 million.[1] So for any readers who watch closely the Chinese capital market, it would certainly be interesting to learn the story behind this fast runner.

---

[1] 2011 Annual Report of Eternal Asia: http://www.cninfo.com.cn

J. G. Wang and J. Yang, *Who Gets Funds from China's Capital Market?*, SpringerBriefs in Business, DOI: 10.1007/978-3-642-44913-0_6, 

## 6.1 An Era of Outsourcing: Non-core Businesses

Any consumer in present-day China can probably talk as to an awareness of the rapid development of online shopping, a sensation that's not only given birth to big-time e-commerce companies such as Taobao and Jingdong, but also gave a huge push to the supporting logistics industry. Fast delivery companies such as EMS, S.F. Express, and San Tong Yi Da,[2] just to name a few, have become well-known household names in recent years. However, the booming of the express delivery business, whose primary function is to transport goods either between businesses and individuals, or between individuals, is just the tip of the iceberg when it comes to the logistics industry. The broad definition of the logistics market also includes the transportation of goods between companies, which has led to the popular concept of a supply chain (Figs. 6.1, 6.2, 6.3, 6.4 and 6.5).

As commonly defined, a supply chain is a system of organizations, people, technology, activities, information or resources involved in moving a product or service from a supplier to a customer. Supply chain activities transform natural resources, such as raw materials and components, into a finished product that is delivered to the end customer. Purchase, transportation, warehousing, distribution, and settlement comprise the major components of a supply chain. In China, where transportation costs have never to date been observed moving down, an efficient logistics and supply chain can help significantly reduce a company's cost of overall business operations.

Given the limited resources that a company may potentially possess, it is sometimes difficult for a firm to set up and maintain a well-run, low-cost supply chain on its own. Most often than not, a company's strength lies in its R&D, production, or sales, rather than in non-core business areas such as logistics or supply chain management. These neglected areas, however, actually cover a wide spectrum of activities including transportation, distribution, warehousing and inventory management, custom clearance, and others. When a firm is still small in scale with a relatively simple business model, its suppliers and sales network are probably relatively easy and straightforward to manage. For these small businesses, it might still be possible for the company to handle its logistics issues on its own. However, as a company grows, its vendor and customer relationships typically become much more complicated, and its supply chain, subsequently, becomes more sophisticated as well. When dealing with multiple suppliers for raw materials and multiple sales channels for products, a company has to tackle new challenges such as optimized transportation route, balanced budget, reasonable inventory level, and efficient distribution. Even coordinating payment settlement to each of its numerous vendors may become a logistical challenge. When a firm's supply chain goes so far as to involve imports and exports, custom clearance becomes another money/time-consuming issue for the firm. The increasing need

---

[2] San Tong Yi Da is an abbreviation of four private express companies in China, namely Yto, Sto, Zto and Yunda.

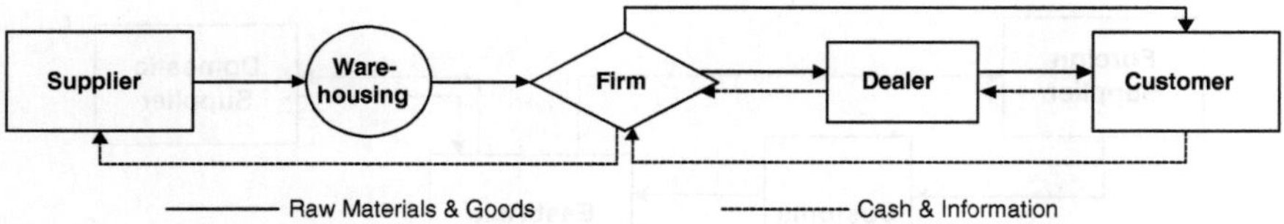


**Fig. 6.1** Supply chain of a company

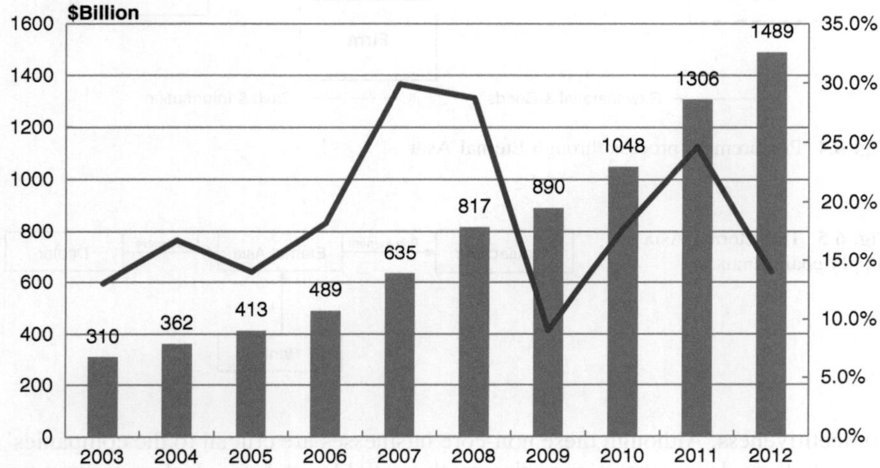


**Fig. 6.2** Expenditure in China's logistics and supply chain management services market (National Bureau of Statistics of China: http://www.stats.gov.cn/. The figures are converted to US dollar using the average exchange rate of the corresponding year.)

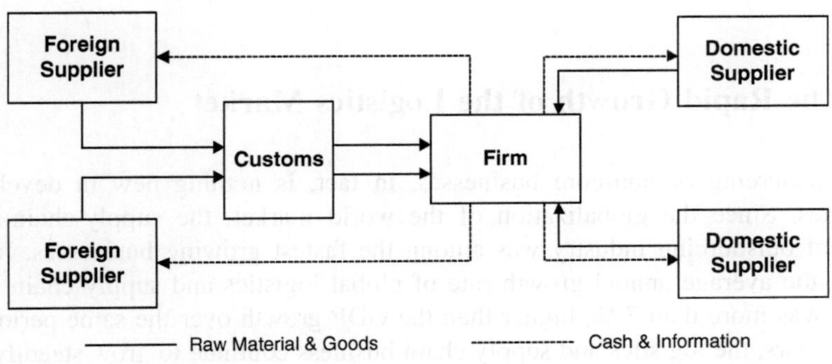


**Fig. 6.3** General procurement process

for competently dealing with non-core businesses meant that if handled by the company itself, these businesses would unavoidably lead to an increase in the company's operating costs and a generally negative impact on the firm's overall

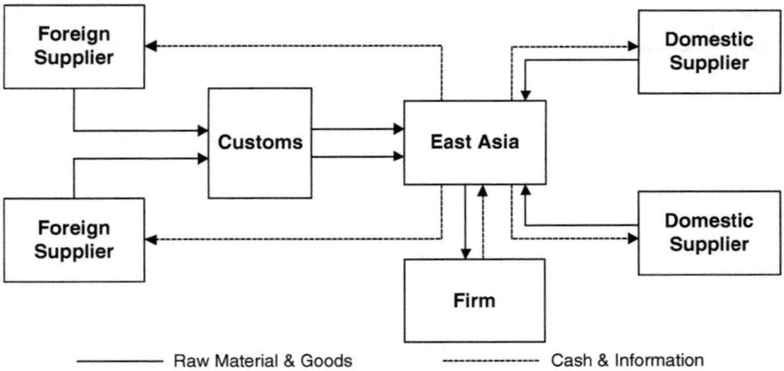


**Fig. 6.4** Procurement process through Eternal Asia

**Fig. 6.5** The Eternal Asia's supply chain financing

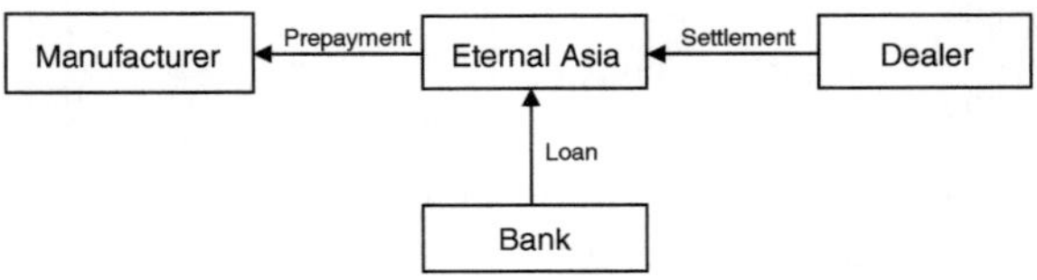


competitiveness. Although these non-core businesses are crucial to the companies' success, they do not have expertise in these fields, and not dealing with these functions enables the company to focus its attention, time and money on the things that they can do best and will be unquestionably of great value. As a result, outsourcing these non-core-businesses to professional logistic firms has become an increasingly popular and increasingly ideal solution.

## 6.2 The Rapid Growth of the Logistics Market

The outsourcing of non-core businesses, in fact, is nothing new in developed countries. Since the globalization of the world market, the supply-chain-management outsourcing industry was among the fastest growing businesses. In the 1990s, the average annual growth rate of global logistics and supply chain businesses was more than 7 %, higher than the GDP growth over the same period. In recent years, the logistics and supply chain business continue to grow steadily at a rate of about 4 % a year.[3]

In emerging markets such as China, the rapid growth of supply chain business is not a surprise as well. As more and more multinational corporations enter into the

[3] Pingan Security Research Report: http://business.sohu.com/20071029/n252925361.shtml

China market, they not only brought over the concept of outsourcing non-core businesses, but they also brought real business volumes of the supply chain management services into China's domestic market. With the over 8 % GDP growth in China's economy, an increasing number of domestic Chinese companies also began to seek outsourcing for their logistics functions in order to reduce costs and improve core competency. In 2006, the total expenditures on logistics and supply chain services by Chinese companies amounted to about $480 billion, and the total logistics and supply chain costs accounted for about 20 % of GDP. From 2000 to 2005, the annual growth rate of China's logistics and outsourcing services of supply chain management reached 25 %. According to data released by National Bureau of Statistics of China, the market value of logistics and supply chain business in China will reach $1,489 billion in 2012, with a compounded annual growth rate of 17 % from 2003 to 2012. China has now become the world's largest logistics/supply chain management services market.[4]

## 6.3 Segment Player vs. One-Stop Shopping Provider?

China's logistics and supply chain management market is mixed with several kinds of participants. By traditional segmentation, there are traditional transportation and warehousing firms, emerging logistics and supply chain outsourcing companies, and finally, foreign logistics and supply chain outsourcing providers. However, if classified by the types of services provided, there are actually four major categories of service providers in China's logistics and supply chain management industry: traditional logistics service providers, procurement service providers, value-added service providers and whole supply chain management providers. They are further described in Table 6.1.

Currently, the majority of China's logistic service providers are still traditional ones, only focusing their business on transportation and warehousing. There are some value-added service providers, but it appears that there is a huge gap between these firms and their foreign counterparts in terms of both quantity and quality for the services provided. In contrast, providers of whole supply chain management service are still rare. However, as more and more companies jump on the outsourcing trend, they more urgently look for a "housekeeper," to take care of all their supply chain-related issues. In this fourth segment of the logistics industry, Eternal Asia truly stood out as a one-stop-shopping logistics and supply chain service provider. The customers only need to dial one number, the number of Eternal Asia, and all of their logistic needs—from procurement, transportation, warehousing to settlement—will be taken care of with the required quality by the mandated deadlines.

[4] National Bureau of Statistics of China: http://www.stats.gov.cn/

**Table 6.1** Classification of logistics and supply chain management service providers

| Enterprise | Service | Profit model | Representative Companies |
| --- | --- | --- | --- |
| Logistics service provider | Mainly provides logistics and transport services | 1. Logistics and transport services fee<br>2. Logistics and transport, warehousing, cargo handling and freight forwarding fee | China Railway Tielong logistics, COSCO shipping, China shipping development, Jinjiang investment, CMST development, Jielee industry, PG logistics |
| Procurement service provider | Acts as a procurement agent for the manufacturer (or dealer), imports raw materials or semi-finished products according to the order | 1. Procurement agent fee (import agent)<br>2. Custom clearance fee, warehousing fee and other income related to procurement or import | Li & Fung group |
| Value-added service provider | Provides marketing support, customer management, and goods management services for producers | 1. Marketing service fee<br>2. Customer management fee, goods management fee and others related to marketing | ImgramMicro, Arrow, Avnet, Tech data, IDS, Digital China |
| Modern logistics and supply chain management general service provider | Provides entire solutions for the design, implementation and operation of an enterprise's distribution, procurement, logistics and supply chain system | 1. Supply chain integration fee<br>2. Supply chain value-added service fee (such as supply chain settlement services) | Eternal Asia, Kerry Logistics, C.H.Robinson, DFDS, UTI Worldwide |

*Source* IPO Prospectus of Eternal Asia

## 6.4 A Rising Star

Originally also a traditional logistics service provider, Eternal Asia made its transition and moved its growth into the fast lane in 2003. During that year, Eternal Asia entered into its first official collaboration agreement with Cisco as a distributor of latter's products in China. As the distributor, Eternal Asia needed to transport goods from overseas and then deliver them to dealers across China. During this project, Eternal Asia underwent on behalf of Cisco all custom clearance procedures, performed the cargo sorting according to Cisco's requirements, and provided Cisco with all the tracking information at the very end.

**Table 6.2** Five major customers of Eternal Asia before IPO (RMB, in million)

| Customer | Products | January–June, 2007 | | 2006 | |
|---|---|---|---|---|---|
| | | Units Sold | Revenue | Units Sold | Revenue |
| Benq | LCD display/laptop/computer components/digital products | 1247.07 | 2.49 | 2340.80 | 5.65 |
| Philips | Display/lighting/multimedia/medical equipment/car audio | 581.42 | 2.45 | 1853.86 | 2.76 |
| Cisco | Network products | 1593.85 | 10.26 | 1809.86 | 12.22 |
| Tsinghua Tongfang | Laptop and PC components | 526.91 | 12.92 | 1198.26 | 27.64 |
| Ingram Micro | Network products and components | 737.59 | 2.96 | 1070.08 | 4.20 |

*Source* IPO Prospectus of Eternal Asia

Through its cooperation with Cisco, one of the world's top 500 corporations, Eternal Asia not only made some big bucks on the financial side, but also learned for the first time the concept and practice of outsourcing non-core businesses. Eternal Asia swiftly identified the tremendous business potentials behind this new business concept, and made a strategic decision to transform the company from a traditional logistic service provider to a professional provider of whole supply chain management services.

Did Eternal Asia make the right decision in its transformation? The data tells the story all on its own. Since its collaboration with Cisco and its repositioning as a one-stop shopping solutions provider, Eternal Asia's business soared. Many large corporations, including several Fortune 500 names, became clients of Eternal Asia, as indicated by the Table 6.2. Eternal Asia's sales increased dramatically from 2.6 billion RMB in 2000 to 18.2 billion RMB in 2006, with a compound annual growth rate of about 38 %. Its gross profit margin was more than 60 % in 2006. Therefore, it was definitely not unexpected that, when Eternal Asia went for its IPO in 2007, it easily raised RMB 770 million with its first day stock price up about 111 %.

## 6.5 A Smart First Move: Catching the Big Fish in Familiar Waters

It is probably fair to say that Eternal Asia's "good luck" started when it got the contract with Cisco, one of 2003's Fortune 500 companies. Since then, Eternal Asia has allocated its many resources on obtaining similarly large multinational clients, and many international big names had been added to Eternal Asia's client list, such as General Electric, AMD, and Philips—just to name a few.

Working with these large clients was indispensable for Eternal Asia's success. On one hand, it exposed Eternal Asia, as mentioned earlier, to critical new business concepts, such as the outsourcing of non-core-business and supply chain management. These new business concepts triggered Eternal Asia's further exploration into the opportunities in China's supply chain management service market and its tremendous potential. It helped Eternal Asia quickly positioned itself in this new market and gain an enormous first-mover advantage.

On the other hand, large international corporations typically have more business needs in more areas of the logistic industry, along with a higher requirement in terms of security, stability and reliability of their supply chain. Multinational corporations are also more involved in imports and exports, thus, have the need for customs clearance processes as well. As a result, working with these large multinational corporations not only provided the volume and the resulting economy of scale for Eternal Asia, but also allowed Eternal Asia to become familiar with the management of every single process in the supply chain. This prepared Eternal Asia well in becoming a one-stop-shopping service provider later on.

Eternal Asia made the smart move of trying to catch the big fish, but in familiar waters first. The company's founder, Zhou Guohui, had run two IT companies before he founded Eternal Asia, and had a solid understanding of and hands on experience in the IT industry. Therefore, Eternal Asia went after big name company contracts, but began by concentrating on the industries it already had some background knowledge of. Zhou and Eternal Asia were able to overcome their newcomer status in the logistics industry by at least focusing on the supply chains of industries they were old hat in—IT, electronics, and medical devices. This move greatly lowered the entry risk for Eternal Asia, and reduced its cost of business operations.

## 6.6 How They Played the Game

To fully understand the value Eternal Asia's solutions presented to its customers, let's take a closer look at the way that traditional logistic service providers typically operated. The traditional supply chain firms offer procurement and distribution services. For procurement, the routing process consisted of a production company, which needed to first send orders to all the raw material suppliers, and then organize transportation, warehousing, and the final settlement separately. When the number of suppliers is large, the maintenance of a strong relationship with each supplier becomes very difficult.

With Eternal Asia's solution, however, the production companies only needed to place orders to Eternal Asia, and Eternal Asia would take care of finishing the orders to various suppliers, handling all the formalities, arranging the transportation of goods, and finally settling the payment. These production companies only need to dial Eternal Asia's number, pay one bill to Eternal Asia, then just wait for the goods to arrive at a pre-determined schedule. This one-stop shopping solution

**Table 6.3** Revenue and profit of Eternal Asia's main business (RMB, in million)

| | January–June, 2007 | 2006 | 2005 | 2004 |
|---|---|---|---|---|
| Revenue from main business | 164.5015 | 284.4084 | 184.7761 | 147.1879 |
| Distribution | 71.9163 | 141.0632 | 112.6593 | 125.8291 |
| Procurement | 92.5852 | 143.3452 | 72.1168 | 21.3588 |
| Operating profit | 68.7129 | 120.4561 | 95.2363 | 84.1708 |
| Total profit | 68.8488 | 123.8909 | 94.9232 | 84.1580 |
| Net profit | 60.6591 | 105.1139 | 83.5473 | 68.4828 |

*Source* IPO Prospectus of Eternal Asia

makes the procurement an easy job, and saves the production companies a tremendous amount of manpower, time and money.

For the distribution of goods, it is a similar story. Under the traditional model, the production company needed to ship the goods to each individual dealer, wholeseller and customer, and make the settlement to each separately. With Eternal Asia's solution, however, the client company needs only to send a single instruction to Eternal Asia, and Eternal Asia will dispatch the products to corresponding dealers and customers and make the settlement on behalf of the production firm. Eternal Asia makes the entire supply chain of the production firm much simpler and more efficient, changing it from one-to-many to a one-to-one model, greatly reducing the cost and time of the production business' operations. Meanwhile, Eternal Asia would earn the service fee for its one-stop-shopping supply chain logistic services, and achieve a win–win result with its customers. As a proof of the success of the model, just look at the growth in Eternal Asia's revenue and profit over this 3-year period, as shown in Table 6.3.

### *6.6.1 The Keys to One-Stop-Shopping: Specialization and Economies of Scale*

Eternal Asia's main advantage, as noted, is its one-stop shopping service. The reason they are able to provide this kind of service over local traditional logistics management providers is by the perfectly seamless integration of a four-in-one business which contains business flow, logistics flow, capital flow and information flow. Traditional companies, no matter a logistics service provider, a procurement service provider or a value-added service provider, all primarily focus on a part of the supply chain, and didn't have the capacity or knowledge to provide efficiency and synergy for the customer. In contrast, Eternal Asia integrated the entire supply chain and even participated in the clients' marketing activities to help collect relevant information and feedback. More specifically, Eternal Asia's menu of services is extremely thorough and comprehensive. Its capabilities are as exhaustive as they might be exhausting to list: import/export customs clearance, international logistics and distribution, domestic logistics and distribution, value-

**Table 6.4** Comparison of Eternal Asia and its traditional counterparts

| Items | Eternal Asia | Logistics service provider | Value-added service provider | Procurement service provider |
|---|---|---|---|---|
| Inventory management | ○ | ○ | ○ | ○ |
| Possessing inventory | × | × | ○ | ○ |
| Accepting orders | ○ | × | ○ | ○ |
| Send orders to suppliers | ○ | × | ○ | × |
| Order from suppliers directly | ○ | × | ○ | ○ |
| Send goods to dealers or customers | ○ | ○ | × | ○ |
| Settlement with dealers or customers | ○ | × | ○ | × |
| Marketing support | ○ | × | ○ | × |
| Customer service management | ○ | × | ○ | ○ |
| Settlement support | ○ | × | ○ | ○ |

*Source* IPO Prospectus of Eternal Asia

added processing, warehousing, special tax treatment zones, international procurement execution, settlement of the supply chain services, vendor managed inventory (VMI), international maintenance centers, and all other ancillary services. It has truly become an all-purpose "housekeeper" that makes its clients' operations worry-free (See Table 6.4 for more details).

Another important aspect to note is the financial aspect of the Eternal Asia's model. On the revenue side, Eternal Asia charges a service fee as a percentage of the transaction, which is usually about 1 to 3 %. On the cost side, Eternal Asia lowers down its operating expenses through specialization. Its bottom line profit is obtained through economy of scale.

In addition, as a professional supply chain management service provider, Eternal Asia possesses a well-trained, professional management team with the needed expertise and resources to address the issues presented by its customers. This management team installed an Enterprise Resource Planning (ERP) system, which enables Eternal Asia to manage all its customers' finance, billing, invoice, cost, logistics, and contracts in a fully digital manner, allowing Eternal Asia to provide customized services to its various clients. It is working both with technology and with skills that peers providing traditional logistics services simply can't compete with.

Finally, by pooling together similar orders from its customers, Eternal Asia can effectively reduce the numbers of orders it had to handle while keeping the value of the total transactions unchanged. For example, raw materials ordered by the same types of companies are usually the same, the nuances of which Eternal Asia learns from experience. It can then systematically and efficiently bundle these orders into one, significantly reducing the number of actual orders it needs to process while reducing cost. More customers from the same industry, more savings on marginal cost for Eternal Asia. This cost advantage gave Eternal Asia an adequate buffer in order to pursue competitive pricing that attracts customers and sustains Eternal Asia's business. Over the years, Eternal Asia has gradually established its dominance in the electronics market, IT market and medical equipment market, all through this economy of scale. These long-run relationships guarantee Eternal Asia with a steady revenue source for years to come.

### *6.6.2 A Game Changer: Supply Chain Financing*

One-stop shopping for all its customers' needs was and still is Eternal Asia's claim to fame, but it really hit the mark as an industry genius when it went even further to financing its customers. Over the years, Eternal Asia has developed an innovative financial model - supply chain financing, to provide funds for the companies in its supply chain. This new business model not only provided significant value for its immediate customers, but also had a tremendous impact on small business financing in general.

Needless to say, every company needs funds to survive and thrive. But this is especially true for small and medium sized enterprises (SMEs). The need for funds may come from many sources, and may go either to the company's long-term capital expenditure or its short-term working capital functioning. For a small business' logistics operations, it typically needs funds for trade credit, accounts receivables, and accounts payables among others. In particular, SMEs desperately need short term financing in order to complete the entirety of its logistical procedures. However, small business financing is a well-known challenging issue worldwide, due to many risky characteristics of SMEs such as asymmetric information, quality of financial statements, or inadequate credit records and history that make them unattractive for many investors. For Eternal Asia, helping its SME customers finance their transactions was certainly a big challenge, but it also represents a great business opportunity. As noted, Eternal Asia quickly acted on this opportunity to develop its supply chain financing strategy.

Eternal Asia's supply chain financing model works like this: For the purchasing process, as the buyers' authorized purchasing agent, Eternal Asia would pay the seller using its own funds through wire transfers, letters of credit or guarantees on behalf of the buyers, collecting payment from the buyers when the goods are finally shipped to the buyers' warehouse. For the distribution process, and for these sellers or distributors (manufacturers), Eternal Asia is usually also their logistic service provider. So when Eternal Asia ships their goods to buyers, it pays in advance on behalf of buyers when the goods leave the sellers' warehouse. So in this case, seller can receive the payment when the goods just leave its warehouse, and reduce the risk of default on payment from the buyer. On the other hand, buyer pays only when they receive the goods, so it reduces the risk of default on goods delivery from the seller end. The prepayment ratio of Eternal Asia for its customers is generally about 20 to 30 % of the total transaction value.

Providing prepayment on behalf of its customers requires a lot of funds up-front, and requires Eternal Asia to bear the risks that it has shifted away from its customers. So the questions are how Eternal Asia can obtain the funds that were needed by its customers (that the customers ordinarily would have to obtain by themselves directly from a financial institution), and how Eternal Asia can mitigate the financial risks that it subsequently exposes itself to. The answer to the first question, for Eternal Asia at least, is getting funds by obtaining loans from banks by leveraging its large scale of business and sound credit records. Compared with its separate SME clients, Eternal Asia itself is a well-established firm, and can much more easily get approval for bank loans than if these SME customers applied themselves. To the banks, lending funds to firms of larger size with more values in collaterals and better credit history is a much safer bet against default risk; as a result, Eternal Asia's model helps its small business customers gain financing by allowing them to "detour" through the core company—Eternal Asia itself.

However, the annual interest rate charged for the loan from banks is usually about 5 to 7 % on average,[5] and Eternal Asia typically only charges 1 to 3 % to its customers. It begs the question, does this model work financially? And how can Eternal Asia afford to borrow money from the bank at a higher interest rate while charging a much lower service fee to the customers that it's providing this "re-financing" for? The key to the issue is the funds turnover ratio, also known as velocity. According to the data provided in Eternal Asia's prospectus, the accounts receivable (AR) turnover of Eternal Asia was about 20 times or more per year. With a business transaction of RMB 5 million, and an interest rate of loan 6 % annually, if Eternal Asia made a 20 % prepayment, as specified in the contract, of 5 million (or RMB 1 million), then the total interest Eternal Asia need to pay to the bank would be RMB 60,000. On the other hand, if Eternal Asia charges a service fee of 2 % of the transaction value of 5 million, with an annual AR turnover of 20 times, Eternal Asia would get 2 million in revenue from the service fee it charged to its customers, which makes the 60,000 interest expense of borrowing from banks rather insignificant.

As for the risks that Eternal Asia is exposed to with the supply chain financing model, an immediate effect is high debt ratio for the firm. As prepayment is funded primarily through bank loans, Eternal Asia's debt ratio was as high as 90 % or above, as indicated by Table 6.5, whereas short-term loans accounted for more than 80 % of total liabilities. If the prepayment could not be recovered on time, then Eternal Asia's liquidity will be jeopardized, it may fail to repay the bank loans and be at risk of bankruptcy.

In general, however, Eternal Asia is in a better position than the bank to mitigate the default risk for financing these SMEs, seeing as it is also the logistics service provider of the cargos of its customers. Eternal Asia can use these goods that it is shipping as collateral against the default risk. Eternal Asia also has much

[5] Calculated from the benchmark rates of short-term loans announced by PBOC: http://www.pbc.gov.cn/

**Table 6.5** Debt ratio of Eternal Asia

| | Jan–Jun 2007 | 2006 | 2005 | 2004 |
|---|---|---|---|---|
| Debt ratio | 91.03 % | 94.28 % | 95.71 % | 93.34 % |

*Source* IPO Prospectus of Eternal Asia

better knowledge than the bank about its customers through its previous transactions with these companies. In particular, to control the risk of default on prepayment and reduce the possible losses due to bad debts, Eternal Asia established a set of procedures for client scrutiny through credit checks, risk assessment, and enhancement of the control system. This "insider" information would be much less thorough or inaccessible by banks.

According to the prospectus of Eternal Asia, customers accepted by Eternal Asia to receive financing are generally the companies of decent size and market share as well as a stable business either at home or abroad. The goods that Eternal Asia selected to carry are usually IT products, medical equipment and other high-valued products that can be relatively easier to sell for cash, mitigating a potential liquidity risk. In addition, for projects that are identified as high risk by pre-screening process, Eternal Asia would assign a project manager to constantly monitor the progress of the project, timely issue early warnings signs, and develop contingency plans to make any needed changes in a timely manner.

### *6.6.3 Ahead of the Game*

In many ways, supply chain financing is a double-edged sword, a high risk but high return business. Eternal Asia bore the high risk and won the return as a result. By providing its customers with prepayment at the signing of the contract, Eternal Asia won over a large number of SMEs that desperately needed financing, and did something that its traditional competitors didn't have the slightest ability to match in the short-term.

In the long run, however, the high entry barrier that Eternal Asia had built in the logistic services industry, especially for procurement and distribution, became less unreachable for other companies, and the supply chain financing model can be copied over time in one way or another. Therefore, to maintain its competitive edges, and realize higher financial values, Eternal Asia has set up a new plan for its further development.

At the core of its new business plan is to establish a trading platform of consumer goods with the direct provisioning system set up in 380 cities across the country. Through this platform, buyers can order whatever they need directly from the suppliers, and manufacturers can also directly supply their products to the dealers or end buyers. This platform would subvert the conventional multi-level-agent sales model, eliminate numerous intermediate layers, and thus, help companies reduce the cost of procurement and sales. With this plan, which was named

"Plan 380", Eternal Asia will further expand its primary business from supply chain management to trading platform operations, develop more customized services to its clients, and establish a global supply chain platform network to provide more value-added services. In addition, Eternal Asia also plans to expand its industry coverage from the current IT, electronics and medical device industry to pharmaceutical, retail and home appliance industries, where Eternal Asia hopes to copy its success in the current industries and generates new spots of growth in the future.

## 6.7 From Private Equity to Public Financing

Every company has its own S-shaped life cycle growth curve. There is also a financial growth cycle that is associated with its physical product growth for the firm. As the fund is the number one necessity for any company, Eternal Asia, for sure, was not an exception. But not only that, as a one-stop shopping logistic service provider and a fund lender of supply chain financing service, Eternal Asia, actually, had an even bigger appetite for funding. But similar to its peers, Eternal Asia also experienced a journey of getting financed taking from owners' own capital at the beginning, to private equity's injection in the middle, and eventually gaining the access to vast public capital market. The major milestones for Eternal Asia were the private equity investment from SAIF Partners and King Express, and its successful IPO in Shenzhen Stock Exchange.

At the end of 2006, attracted by Eternal Asia's unique business model and its tremendous potential, SAIF Partners, a private equity fund, invested USD $18.22 million in Eternal Asia, and in return, obtained 22.27 % shares of the company. At about the same time, King Express, another private equity fund, put another $1 million into Eternal Asia, and acquired 1.22 % of the company's stake. These large capital inflows helped Eternal Asia timely "balanced" its balance sheet, and provided the firm with its badly needed funding to support the implementation of Eternal Asia's money-consuming business model. On the other hand, Eternal Asia also did not disappoint its investors. One year after the listing of the Eternal Asia, the gain for these private equity funds on Eternal Asia's stock was nearly 800 % if using the first day opening price of 52 RMB as the bench mark!

In November 2007, Eternal Asia successfully got listed in the Shenzhen Stock Exchange. The company issued 31 million shares of common stock at a price of RMB 24.89, which brought in RMB 730 million's cash for the company. After IPO, the original founder Zhou, Guo Hui remained as the majority owner with 56.4 % shares of Eternal Asia through two of his fully controlled firms, Shenzhen Union Digital Holding Co., Ltd and Shenzhen Union Elite Technology Co., Ltd. SAIF Partners still stayed on the shareholders' list with 5.39 % shares, ranked the number 3 largest shareholder, after Shenzhen Union Digital Holding Co., Ltd and Shenzhen Union Elite Technology Co., Ltd. The remaining 38.21 % of Eternal Asia shares were held by many individual investors from general public. Eternal

Asia's IPO was truly a success. As mentioned at the beginning, on the first day of trading, its stock price rose by 111 % with a P/E ratio as high as 63 times! Without a question, Eternal Asia's potential for the future, which was supported by its innovative business model, was strongly endorsed by the investors in China's capital market.

# Chapter 7
# The Bird of First Light: The Story of Sunbird Yacht

**Abstract** The luxury goods industry is another emerging market in China. In particular, yachts are among the hottest new products in luxury good consumption, attracting many companies to enter and play in the market. However, one of the challenges of operating in the industry lies in the highly customized nature of the end products, making it difficult for companies to gain economies of scale and be profitable. Sunbird, the leading yacht maker whose case will be discussed in this chapter, developed a modulated business infrastructure that combined standardization of production with customization in design.

**Keywords** Luxury goods market · Yacht industry · Economy of scale · Customized industry · Branding

The burgeoning luxury goods industry in China is attracting worldwide attention from luxury manufacturers, enthusiasts and investors alike. According to the 2012 "China Luxury Market Study", a market analysis report released by Bain and Company,[1] China's luxury goods market experienced a 20 % growth in 2012 (as expressed by Euros). Just as Chinese consumers have become the largest consumer group for the luxury goods worldwide, the Greater China area has also replaced Japan as the second largest luxury goods market. Among these luxury goods, yachts were widely considered as one of the foremost markets with the potential to take off in the next decade. In 2008, China imported from Italy, US, UK and other countries over 1,900 boats and yachts with a total value over $50 million. On the export side, China exported boats and yachts with values from $180 million in 2007 to $260 million in 2009, chronicling China's entry into the top bracket of yacht makers worldwide.

This chapter's story is about Sunbird, a leading firm in China's yacht industry. Its full company name is Hunan Sunbird Yacht Manufacture Co., Ltd., and it was established in Yuanjiang City, Hunan in 1993. Compared with its peers, who were primarily traditional, low-end, "made-in-China" type of manufacturers, Sunbird Yacht was a modern marvel. In addition to its unique business model and well-

[1] Bain & Company: http://www.bain.cn/news.php?act=show&id=407

J. G. Wang and J. Yang, *Who Gets Funds from China's Capital Market?*, SpringerBriefs in Business, DOI: 10.1007/978-3-642-44913-0_7, 

maintained government relations, its exceptional design and innovative ability also made Sunbird a well-known brand in China's yacht market. They were early birds in a budding industry, and were well-compensated for their successful efforts. In 2010, Sunbird successfully went public through an IPO and became a publicly traded company listed in the Shenzhen Stock Exchange (Ticker: 300123), raising over 600 million RMB.[2] Let's take a look at this intriguing story in the following sections to uncover what it is about Sunbird that makes it a shining beacon on China's lucrative waterways.

## 7.1 Not All Boats Are Yachts

Privilege is fact in this industry—not all water-faring vehicles can be called yachts. According to the international standard, only leisure boats with a length of over 10 m and a price of over $100,000 can be defined as a yacht, and all others that fall outside of these criteria are merely called boats. Out of mainland China, the definition of yacht is usually any appliance or equipment with a length of no less than 2.5 m, and used as a "mobile water device for non-profit purposes such as marine sports, fishing or entertainment".[3] In mainland China, the official definition of yacht as defined by China's Ministry of Transportation (MOT) is "a boat with a motor, and is only used by its owners for sightseeing, leisure and entertainment activities".[4]

Delving even deeper, the yacht industry in China can actually be further divided into three subcategories: private yacht, commercial yacht and special-purpose yacht. A private yacht is one that is only used by its owners for sightseeing, leisure and entertainment activities, and its owner must obtain a certificate issued by the Ship Inspection Department of the Chinese government. A commercial yacht is a yacht that can accommodate more than 12 people, and is used for profit and business activities. Owners of these yachts must also obtain certificates from the inspection department, either as a cruise ship or a passenger ship. Because the practice of private yacht ownership in China is still in its embryonic stage, 80 % of the 1,200 officially registered yachts are commercial yachts owned by government or tourism companies. Finally, special-purpose yachts are those used for law enforcement on the water, port pilotage, hydrographic surveys, scientific research, flood relief, and military.

---

[2] Eastmoney Data Center: http://data.eastmoney.com/xg/xg/detail/300123.html

[3] For example, Macau's Regulation 82/99M.

[4] China's Ministry of Transportation: http://www.gov.cn/flfg/2008-08/13/content_1070955.htm

## 7.2 Late Bloomers: China's Yacht Industry

The development of the yacht industry in China only began in the late 1970s as China started to develop its shipbuilding industry. Since then, it has gone through three episodes of growth: The first one was its nascent stage, marked by the homegrown production of low-end yachts. In the late 1970s, before the period of social reform and open-door policy in China, the concept of private yachts did not yet exist. There only existed a few commercial yachts, such as paddle boats, motor boats and tour boats that could be seen in water parks, beaches, or other public entertainment facilities that had bodies of water. Changzhou FRP Shipyard was considered the earliest yacht manufacturer in China, primarily engaging in the manufacturing of glass fiber reinforced plastic (FRP) yachts. Even today, it is still among the top ten yacht makers in China.

The second period was the main take-off period of the yacht industry in China, with collaborations alongside foreign yacht manufacturers to produce much higher-end yachts. From the 1980s to the early 1990s, as China gradually opened up to the global market and started to develop its tourism industry, yacht manufacturers from the United States, Japan, Hong Kong and Taiwan began to collaborate with the FRP shipyard manufacturers in mainland China. Interactions included collaborations in as processing or technical and management consulting, tech transfer, joint ventures, even the setting up of some wholly foreign-owned companies. During this period of time, China's FRP shipyard manufacturers produced for the first time vehicles like sail boats, fishing boats and family-used leisure boats, all using imported raw materials and equipment under European and U.S. standards.

The third stage was one of independent design. At the arrival of the twenty-first century, China's yacht industry was seeing some significant changes. First, as the concept of yacht consumption burgeoned, many successful businessmen in China began dabbling in yacht consumption as part of their leisure activities, and various yacht clubs also sprung up nationwide. As a result, a new domestic yacht market in China emerged. By November 2006, there were nearly 300 yacht manufacturing companies in China, about 60 yacht clubs, and the annual sales revenue of the whole yacht manufacturing industry climbed over RMB 1 billion. Meanwhile, China-made yachts were being exported to more than 70 countries, to the point where exports accounted for over 60 % of the total yacht sales in China.

Another change was that Chinese yacht makers started to make yachts using their own intellectual property rights in that period of time, embracing the concept of branding. During 2008, the Beijing Olympics selected one of the premier brands of yachts to exclusively design large luxury yachts used for water sports. That brand was Sunbird Yacht.

The yachts that Sunbird made for the Olympics were truly made-and-designed-in-China products with fully independent intellectual property rights. They combined leading exterior design concepts from Western luxury yachts with traditional Chinese influences regarding interior space and structure. Their yachts combined the functionality of a cruise with the appeal of vehicles used in inland rivers, lakes and coastal waters for sports, entertainment, sightseeing, business meetings and other water activities. It was truly a mobile maritime palace, priced at almost half of the tag on foreign yachts of the same grade.

## 7.3 Who Are the Players in the Water

In an attempt to capture the fast growing luxury goods market in China, the yacht market in China is highly concentrated and competitive. Depending upon the segment, the players vary slightly in function and type. The high end of the luxury yacht market is pretty much just a show room for big foreign names such as Sunseeker and Princess of Britain, Reviera of Australia, Beneteau of France, Ferretti and Azimut of Italy, and Bavaria of Germany. By 2008, all of them had set up office in China. However, due to the high price bracket of these brands, demand for these yachts is still limited, at least for the time being.

In the middle-to-high-end market, however, there is intense competition between domestic and foreign brands, and Sunbird, Brunswick (U.S.), Xianli (Hong Kong), Jieteng (Taiwan), and Shanghai Double Happiness Yacht, the top players in this bracket, constantly vie for customers within the segment. Among them, Xianli and Jieteng primarily export yachts, while Sunbird, Changzhou FRP Shipbuilding and a few other firms dominate the special-purpose yacht market. The latter receive orders from high-end customers such as China's State Oceanic Administration (SOA), Customs, Port Pilotage Stations, and certain military institutions.

The last market segment of the yacht industry consists of multi-purpose speedboats and assault boats and is characterized by a high degree of product homogeneity. These boats tend to be produced by a large number of low-end manufacturers.

The output value of the major yacht makers in China's yacht market in 2008 is summarized in Table 7.1.

## 7.4 A Golden Waterway

It is clear to China's luxury goods market observers that the yacht market in China holds great potential in the years to come. Several factors contribute to this projection of future growth. The first is China's ideal geological nature. China is a country with numerous lakes, islands, and rivers. It boasts 18,000 km of coastline (including 14,000 km of island coastline), 3 million km$^2$ economic sea areas, 24,800 lakes, the four major rivers (Yangtze River, Yellow River, Pearl River, and

**Table 7.1** Output value of China's major yacht enterprises in 2008

| Industry ranking | Enterprise name | Main products | Output value in 2008 (RMB in million) |
|---|---|---|---|
| 1 | Xianli (Zhuhai) Shipbuilding Co., Ltd. | Yachts, engineering boats | 280 |
| 2 | Sunbird Yacht Co., Ltd. | Composite material private yachts, business yachts, special yachts | 165.83 |
| 3 | Dongguan Jieteng Shipbuilding Co., Ltd. | Tug yachts | 140 |
| 4 | Zhuhai Jianglong Shipbuilding Co., Ltd. | Composite material special yachts, fishing boats, yachts | 120 |
| 5 | Guangdong Poly Marine & Engineering Co., Ltd. | Small tug yachts, sports fishing yachts, law enforcement yachts for the Customs | 102.8 |
| 6 | Zhuhai Sunloong Shipyard Co., Ltd. | Composite material special yachts, fishing boats, yachts | 101.4 |
| 7 | Shanghai Double Happiness Yacht Company | Yachts, sailing boats | 92.1 |
| 8 | Changzhou FRP Shipbuilding Enterprise | Composite material special yachts, fishing boats, large FRP products and unsaturated polyester resin | 91.7 |
| 9 | Shanghai Baodao Yacht Co., Ltd. | Composite material yachts | 91 |
| 10 | Wuxi Dongfang High Speed Craft Development Co.,Ltd. | Yachts, water recreational devices | 45 |

*Source* China Association of The National Shipbuilding Industry, Boat & Yacht Branch Commission

Heilongjiang River), and more than 6,000 islands.[5] The resplendent water environment of the country is certain to support the burgeoning yacht culture in China.

The second factor is China's fast and stable economic growth for the past three decades. The Chinese's rapid accumulation of wealth and subsequent consumption power is sure to propel the fast development of the yacht industry. If we use what happened in Europe and the United States as an indicator, when a country's GDP per capita reaches USD $3,000, the yacht industry begins to grow, and when the GDP per capita reached $6,000, the yacht industry enters a stage of rapid development. In 2008, China's GDP was $31,404 billion, while GDP per capita had reached $3,000 on average nationwide, and GDP per capita in China's most developed areas such as Yangtze River Delta, Pearl River Delta, and Bohai Rim

5 Ministry of Land and Resources of the People's Republic of China: http://www.mlr.gov.cn

had reached or passed \$8,000.[6] All these economic indicators suggest that the demand and purchasing power for yachts in China are already in place.

Yachts have become particularly popular with affluent Chinese in recent years. According to a survey, individuals with more than RMB 10 million investable assets in China reached about 300,000 in 2008, and among them, at least 5 % of these millionaires expressed their plan to buy a yacht in the near future. If the average price of a yacht is about RMB 2–3 million, the potential market size of total private yachts in China would amount to RMB 30–45 billion, with the compounded annual growth rate of China's yacht market expected to exceed 50 % within the next 5 years.[7]

The top bracket of Chinese can buy yachts like it is almost nothing, but how about the middle class or upper middle class? Actually, for those who can't afford to own a yacht, there is the option of leasing, just like an apartment. Leasing a yacht frees one from the large sum of money required to purchase and maintain the yacht, and the option allows more of the middle class to get to know yachts which greatly promotes yacht consumption on the whole. Therefore, the market potential of China's yacht industry could be far more than even what forecasters project now.

The third factor is the evolution of leisure consumption and the corresponding culture that emerges. In Western countries, the yacht has become a piece of leisure equipment whose popularity nowadays is rivaled only by private jets. With yachts, people can surf, dive, swim, and fish and experience a form of instant escapism from the hectic nature of corporate life. People also use yachts to inspire their sense of adventure with activities such as nautical travelling, global travelling, exploring the sea, and challenging human limits against the forces of nature. But yachting is a brand new concept in China's history and culture, and the mass consumption culture of yachts takes time to cultivate

Chinese civilization, in general, is associated with "land culture" while yachting represents "ocean culture". Comparatively speaking, land culture is a somewhat more closed culture while a marine one reflects a freer and more open lifestyle, of which yachting is an extension. There are fundamental differences between the two. Due to the abundance of inland farming and the corresponding cultural mindset that had developed in China over the last thousands of years, it may take some time for the people of China to understand and adapt an element of marine culture. However, this particular element of marine culture, the yacht industry, is among those attracting increasingly more attention among the Chinese, fulfilling the desires of the glamorous, and is now one of the most promising industries in China.

---

[6] China Statistical Year Book 2009, by National Bureau of Statistics of China: http://www.stats.gov.cn

[7] China Merchants Bank, Bain & Company: China Private Wealth Report 2011: http://www.bain.cn/news.php?act=show&id=346

A fourth factor is increasingly favorable government regulations. In Western countries, yachts can sail freely cross a nation's waters without entry barriers between different states. In mainland China, however, yacht regulation is not well established. Even yachts from Hong Kong and Macao that can sail freely anywhere else in the world can't sail freely around the mainland coast. In mainland China, the waterways are primarily designed for commercial use such as transportation, and the use of yachts for sports, leisure, and recreation were seldom considered in the past. This situation results in the lack of yacht regulations in mainland China and seriously hampered the development of yacht industry.

Now, though, conditions are changing. On December 1st, 2009, China's State Council issued a paper called "*Opinion on Accelerating the Development of Tourism*", which aimed develop the tourist industry into one of the strategic pillar industries of the national economy, and suggested for the first time to "*support appropriate areas of cruise and yacht tourism, including cruises, yachts and other travel equipment manufacturing industry into the national encouraged-industry directory*".[8] Procedures for yacht-operator training, examination and certification in China were issued on June 14, 2011, which set up a standard for obtaining national yacht driver certification, and makes cross-region yacht navigation possible in the near future.[9]

### 7.4.1 An Early Bird with Great Ambitions

"Designing and manufacturing yachts that Chinese consumers can afford," a quote used by Yuexian Li, the owner of Sunbird, to describe why he started the company. In 1993, the then 30-year-old Li established Hunan Sunbird Yacht Manufacture Co., Ltd. in his hometown of Yuanjiang City, in Hunan Province. At that time, Sunbird was mainly engaged in the development and production of speedboats that were made of new composite material. Yuexian Li really knew nothing about yachts, and actually established the firm believing that yachts and speedboats were same thing.

It wasn't until 1998 that Mr. Li had his first encounter with yachts in Shanghai. By 2000, Sunbird was already exploring production possibilities for small 20–30-foot yachts. In 2003, the company set up its first production facility in Zhuhai that specialized in the production of large yachts. The year of 2005 was a turning point for Sunbird. Although there were no orders from any buyers yet for the vehicle, the company independently designed and manufactured its first large-sized 80-foot yacht in Hunan. The water test for the vehicle turned out to be very successful, and

---

[8] The Central Government of P. R. China: http://www.gov.cn/zwgk/2009-12/03/content_1479523.htm

[9] Maritime Safety Administration of P. R. China: http://www.msa.gov.cn/

the model thrived the minute it hit the market for buyers. Even now, sales for that particular model are still extremely hot.

In 2007, Sunbird Yacht hit another milestone when it entered into the European market, and started to sell its yachts there. The company effectively combined direct domestic sales with the use of foreign agents for overseas markets, bringing in streaming orders to Sunbird.

From 2008 to 2010, the company's revenue was RMB 141, 181 and 244 million, respectively, with an average growth rate of up to 38.6 %. Its domestic customers, which include state-owned companies and owners of private companies, accounted for about one-third of the total sales. From a product sales perspective, yachts in general (commercial yachts plus private yachts) accounted for about 60 % of the company's total revenue, and special-purpose boats accounted for about 40 %. Sunbird's private yachts, in particular, are showing a rapid growth in recent years, as their share increased from 2.8 % in 2007 to 10 % in 2009, making up 20.4 % of sales in the first half of 2010.[10]

On August 24, 2010, China's SEC approved Sunbird's issuing 22 million A-shares at price RMB 28.88 per share. The total funds raised were RMB 635.36 million.[11] After the IPO, Sunbird expanded from purely sales and service of composite material boats to offering a full range of customized solutions from design, manufacturing to maintenance service for its customers. A number of Sunbird's yachts, such as China's first 118-feet catamaran yacht that CITIC Shipping Company ordered as a sightseeing boat for the 2010 Shanghai World Expo and an 80-feet luxury yacht bought by Huawei, represented the highest level of yacht manufacturing in China.

## 7.5 What Made Sunbird Stand Out

A number of factors allowed Sunbird stand out from its competitors. The first notable one is its unique design that integrated Chinese culture with international style. In the yacht industry, design is a defining trait for any yacht maker, directly impacting not just the aesthetics but also the quality, performance and efficiency of a yacht. In general, designing is the weak point for most Chinese yacht makers, and, in particular, there is a large gap between the exterior design of Chinese yachts when measured up against international standards. Part of the problem is the lack of well-trained professional designers in China.

As a matter of fact, not until 2010 did the yacht design major appear for the first time in China's universities. Prior to that, though it is true even today, many domestic yacht manufacturers relied primarily on European and American designers for their yachts, or simply purchased design drawing from research

[10] Sunbird Yacht Co., Ltd, Annual Report 2008–2012.

[11] http://app.finance.ifeng.com/data/stock/tab_gsjj.php?symbol=300123

institutions across China. In addition, compared with the yachts of western countries such as Italy, China's yacht design were much less stylish in appearance.

However, Sunbird was an exception. From the very early stage of its establishment, Sunbird devoted great efforts, in terms of funding and human resource, to the original design of their yachts. The R&D center of Sunbird was also named Hunan Modern Yacht Technology and Industrial Design Center, and was the first provincial level yacht design center in China. It had the largest design team and represented the highest level of development nationwide. As of today, Sunbird has obtained 18 industrial design patents, 3 new model patents, and has 15 patent applications in process. It has designed a series of yachts with the unique Sunbird style, and its yachts have won several domestic design awards including the 2009 China Red Star Design Award, which is one of the most influential awards in industrial design in China, with Sunbird being the only award winner from the shipbuilding industry.

The second factor was its continuous Innovation through its collaboration with research institutions and universities. Sunbird's yacht design center was a joint venture with Hunan University, and Sunbird had technology collaboration agreements with Wuhan Institute of Shipbuilding Technology and several other universities. They jointly developed teaching materials for the education and training of yacht design professionals, who subsequently joined Sunbird's design team. Sunbird also became the test lab for boats made from new materials for Huazhong University of Science and Technology, a top technology institute in China, which allowed Sunbird to develop new composite materials for marine industry.

Through years of exploration, experience, and continued capital investment in R&D, Sunbird significantly enhanced its innovation capability. Combined with its collaboration with leading technology institutions in China, Sunbird also successfully maintained its leading edge in the areas of boat design, materials use, and production process. Up to December 31, 2011, Sunbird had a total of 79 patents, including 1 invention patent, 31 new model patents, and 47 industrial design patents. Among them, 44 were new patents obtained in 2011 alone, which included the one invention patent, 3 new model patents, and 20 industrial design patents. On top of that, Sunbird had 20 patent applications in process in 2010, and 98 in 2011. Sunbird was not only recognized by yacht industry, but also by the defense industry as a designated equipment manufacturer.

The third factor was Sunbird's unique "wholesale" operation model. The yacht industry is very much a customized industry. The features of yacht production are small quantity, large variety, and most yacht makers follow a small-scaled production model. As a consequence, it is difficult for manufacturers in this industry to capture economy of scale, leading to high costs. However, Sunbird innovatively paved a new path in manufacturing by developing a new operation model of integrating personalized design with standardized production—"Scale + Customization".

Like all yacht makers, Sunbird needs large-scaled production to improve its profitability. As early as in 2000, Yuexian Li, the owner of Sunbird visited

Brunswick, Azimut, Ferretti, Yamaha and other internationally renowned yacht makers on a reconnaissance tour, and found that the world's best yacht design was in Europe. The largest market on the whole was in the U.S., and the most efficient production was in Japan. While Li was incredibly impressed by how advanced European and American yacht design was, Li also discovered that their productions were not large in scale, and their management and production models were not very mature either, unlike the productions in Japan.

Thus, Sunbird saw the opportunity for itself: if it could combine the advantages of the yacht designs of Europe, America and Japan, seize the middle class consumer segments, and develop a large-scaled-customized model, they would be able to capture the late-comer advantage. In order to do so, Sunbird first standardized and modulated parts of yacht production as much as possible to eliminate redundant labor and material costs, which also increased the flexibility of their manufacturing. On the other hand, Sunbird prepared over 1,000 sets of yacht design options for customer selection, encompassing almost every possible consumer need. They supplemented this with a customized marketing strategy to strengthen the interactive relationship with the customers. By doing this, Sunbird was able to successfully resolve the dilemma of customized demand versus scaled production.

The fourth successful factor was Sunbird's strong brand building. Having strong design quality and competitive pricing means nothing if the company isn't able to deliver that message to the target customers in a substantial and memorable way. Branding is also critical in creating consumer loyalty to the company's products. In this regard, Sunbird did an excellent job. It first started building name recognition through a simple but effective marketing slogan of "Where there is water, there is Sunbird," encouraging consumers to think of the brand and the ocean itself as companions. To substantiate the claim, Sunbird also vocally publicizes the many titles it has won in the past years, including its Best Asian Yacht Manufacturer nomination in 2008, and its win for Most Influential Chinese Yacht Brand in 2009. It's also very vocal about its strong government connections, which in China is no small feat. In China's domestic market, Sunbird has become the official contracted manufacturer of a number of high-end government and corporate clients such as the Ministry of Transportation, the Ministry of Public Security, and the China Marine Surveillance; its high-profile corporate clients include Huawei, China Jin Mao Group, CITIC Shipping Company and others. Finally, Sunbird distinguished itself by marketing its international presence and attitude towards yacht making. Since Sunbird successfully entered into international markets such as Europe and the United States, and set up subsidiaries in Italy and the US, it used their cultural knowledge to truly brand themselves as a global yacht manufacturer.[12]

[12] Data Source: Trademark Office of the State Administration for Industry & Commerce of the People's Republic of China: http://sbj.saic.gov.cn

The fifth factor contributing to Sunbird's success is their well-maintained government relations. Government relation in China is one of the key factors for success for companies in every industry. Amicable relations and strong ties with the right government agencies not only help a firm go through all the required procedures smoothly and obtain approvals in a timely manner, but they also may provide a firm with tremendous business opportunities via government purchasing. Even though, the privately owned companies had grown from almost zero to more than 50 % of the China's GDP in the last 30 years, state owned business still take up about half of China's economy, and represent the most powerful buyers in the market place. Sunbird understood this perfectly, and made all the right calls.

At the corporate level, Sunbird actively participated in many government or semi-government organizations. It is a member of the Chinese Small Boats Standardization Committee, it takes up the vice-chairman unit of the China Yacht Association, and it is also a member of the Cruise & Yacht Branch of China Transportation Association, the China Shipbuilding Industry Association, the China Fishing Boats and Fishing Machinery Industry Association; the list goes on and on. It even holds the vice-chairman unit of the Hunan New Material Industry Association, and has been appointed to the National Small Vessels Activation Center by the National Economic Activation Center Office.

Sunbird's Chairman Yuexian Li himself, along with his executive board members, are also prolific on an individual level with their activities with government agencies. Li is a member of the Composite Materials Group of the China National Standardization Committee, and he is a part of the China Composite Materials Industry Association. Sunbird's board member Shuxi Liu was the former General Manager of a state-owned company, and a committee member of the Boat Branch of China Shipbuilding Industry Association. The company's independent director Xinfa Yang is the vice president and the secretary-general of the Shanghai Association of Shipbuilding Industry, deputy secretary-general of China Shipbuilding Industry Association, and chairman of the Boat Branch of China Shipbuilding Industry Association since 2001.

The exhaustive list of government agency activity has rewarded Sunbird with huge business benefits in terms of purchasing orders, research projects, grants, and tax benefits. As an example, in December 2010, Sunbird signed "The Construction Contract of Speedboats for Island Protection Law Enforcement" with State Oceanic Administration, a contract worth RMB 271.592 million. In November 2011, Sunbird won another bid with the State Oceanic Administration for a construction contract for speed boats used by China Marine law enforcement, which was worth RMB 215.622 million. In July 2012, Sunbird and its wholly-owned subsidiary Guangdong Poly Marin signed a RMB 110 million contract of special boats with China's General Administration of Customs; just a month later in early August, Sunbird won yet another bid for ultra-high-speed motorboats contract of RMB 15.66 million.[13]

---

13 Prospectus of Sunbird Yacht Company Limited, Announcements: http://www.cnsunbird.com

In addition to commercial contracts, Sunbird also received many grants and much research funding from the Chinese government. For examples, the Continuous Basalt Fiber Reinforced Resin Composite Material & Boat Project that Sunbird conducted in order to develop its patents was fully funded by a national research grant. In 2009, the Commercialization of New Composite Basalt Fiber Reinforced Material Boats project was listed in the first batch of projects to receive financial assistance from the central government. Two years earlier in 2007, a new energy saving, environmentally friendly boat designed by Sunbird was declared a "Hunan Torch Plan Project", the highest level of research projects with government funding.

Furthermore, Sunbird also actively participated in setting important industry standards, such as the standard for Anchoring, Mooring and Dragging Point of Small Boats, "The Classification of High-Speed Inland Water Ships and Standard of Construction", and "The Classification of High-speed Marine Boat and Standard of Construction". In 2009 alone, Sunbird received a total of RMB 3.21 million in subsidies from the government for project funding, IPO funding, and high-tech subsidies. On December 2008, Sunbird was classified as a high-tech company, allowing it to be placed in the 15 % bracket of taxable income instead of the usual corporate 33 % (see footnote 14).

### *7.5.1 The Capital Market: Giving Sunbird Wings*

As with any successful company, Sunbird's growth was not possible without the fund support from capital market. Since its inception, Sunbird had been receiving equity investments continuously from various financial sources. At the beginning, this included the firm owner's own equity investment, individual investors' investment, and private equity. Prior to the IPO, the founder Yuexian Li held over 50 % of the Sunbird's shares through a holding company, Hunan Fengchao, which was under the control of Mr. Li. These shares were held directly by Mr. Li as an individual shareholder. Six other individual investors directly held about 30 % of the shares outstanding, and yet other 13 individual investors jointly held 42 % shares of Hunan Fengchao, the holding firm. The remaining 20 % or so of the Sunbird's shares were held by 5 private equity funds/institutional investors—DaChen Wealth Management (9.23 %), ShenZhen ShengQiao (3.33 %), Suzhou ChuangDongFang (3.33 %), Changsha Huiquan (3.33 %), and Dachen Wealth and Trust (2.52 %).[14]

The funds from the capital markets provided Sunbird with options and choices for its development that would be completely unavailable for companies lacking similar capital backing. One example is the option for Sunbird to expand overseas.

---

[14] Prospectus of Sunbird Yacht Company Limited: http://www.csrc.gov.cn/pub/zjhpublic/cyb/cybypl/201007/P020100730550203127239.pdf

As previously described, China's yacht market possesses huge potential, but it may need a few more years to really take off. The global yacht market, on the other hand, is much larger and can provide Sunbird with short-term cash flows. Sunbird has already started to set up its physical presence overseas, such as their subsidiary Marco Polo in Italy. Meanwhile, Sunbird planned to invest RMB 22 million in its subsidiary Plandy, which it owns in whole, in Hong Kong to support its expansion in Hong Kong and in the rest of the world.

Another advantage provided by the capital markets is government purchasing. With the increasing attention paid by the Chinese government towards the protection of coast lines and disputed islands in deep seas, the demand for special-purpose boats from government agencies is expected to grow exponentially in the next a few years. It just so happens that design and production of special-purpose boats are a few of Sunbird's main strengths.

Another attractive option for Sunbird is merger and acquisition. On a global level, yachts are still considered in large part as handmade products—difficult to enlarge the size of production, and difficult to gain economy of scale. In particular, the industry is quite scattered, segment-wise, with both high-end and relatively low-end customers. Merger and acquisition could potentially be an effective way to integrate the industry and provide a more large-scaled platform in order to fully utilize Sunbird's "customization plus standardization" operation model. With adequate cash in hand via the capital markets, along with numerous target companies in the market place, a horizontal merger and acquisition could pave a new path for Sunbird's continued growth in the future.

The yacht service market could also open another door for Sunbird. Yacht consumption as a leisure activity is becoming more and more popular in more consumer segments, and the yacht service market such as yacht clubs have the potential to become prolific mushroomed in China. Sunbird can consider stepping into this market by vertically integrating to further expand its value chain, either by M&A with existing yacht clubs or by setting up new clubs. Through this vertical integration, Sunbird may be able to maintain at least 30–40 % of its compounded annual revenue growth for the next few years.

Considering this combination of factors, it comes no surprise at all that Sunbird had a successful IPO in 2010. As the bird of the first light, Sunbird can fully take advantage of its early mover status in China. Its business model has pretty much everything it needs to grow in the yacht industry in China, and is in the right position at the right time. As China continues its fast growth, the middle class correspondingly continues to grow, and yacht consumption will become increasingly more popular and affordable as a leisure activity. As for Sunbird, it will continue to fly over China's golden waterway, and investors worldwide would be blind to miss the enormous business opportunities it brings.

# Chapter 8
# The Era of "Designed in China": The Story About Alpha Animation

**Abstract** After 30 years development, China's traditional manufacturing companies are facing the pressure and challenge of China's role—upgrade from low-end manufacturing to the upper ends of industry supply chains. Alpha Animation, one of the top Chinese toy makers whose case will be discussed in this chapter, used their strategic business model to create a path that helped them complete the transfer from a "Made in China" company to a "Designed in China" company.

**Keywords** Toys market · Animation · Made-in-China · Transformation · Cross-media integration

For youngsters born in China in the 1980s, the animated figures that they grew up with, such as the Blue Spirit, Astro Boy, and Sailor Moon, were pretty much all of foreign origin. Even though there were a few notable Chinese animated figures, such as Nezha and Monkey King, they all seemed stiff in image and, to Chinese kids, considerably less attractive than their foreign counterparts. As a result, almost all the toys that Chinese children played within back in those days were Transformers in its various forms.

Animation, however, is widely perceived by social psychologists as an important channel by which a nation can personify the essences of its culture. As China's GDP hit second in the world in the last three decades, the rise of China's indigenous animated figures seems to perfectly complement China's ambitions for a "renaissance" of its 5000-year-long culture. In this regard, the emergence of Alpha Animation may signify the attempt of Chinese animation companies in the recent years to recapture this lost ground.

Alpha Animation's full company name is Guangdong Alpha Animation and Culture Co., Ltd. The firm was established in 1993, and went public on the Shenzhen Stock Exchange in 2009 (Ticker: 002292). At the very beginning, born in the "Made-in-China" age of low priced Chinese manufacturing, Alpha Animation, like most of its contemporary peers, primarily manufactured traditional toys in a traditional Original-Entrusted-Manufacturing (OEM) way. It was simply a regular toy manufacturer, and a part of the "Made in China" cohort. After more than a decade of development, however, Alpha Animation has risen to the top of

J. G. Wang and J. Yang, *Who Gets Funds from China's Capital Market?*,
SpringerBriefs in Business, DOI: 10.1007/978-3-642-44913-0_8, 

animated design in China, and has emerged as a leader of China's toy industry as well. The evolution of the company is not only a self-contained success story, but in fact reflects the dynamics of the global toy industry and the transformation of China's toy makers in the last couple of decades. In particular, Alpha's story illuminates the role played by animated toys and its related products in this historical period of growth in China's toy industry.

For fully understanding the implications of the Alpha's rising for China's toy industry, let's first take a look at what happened in the global and China's toy market in the past years.

## 8.1 Made in China, Designed Elsewhere: The Global Toys Industry

An old Chinese saying once stated that no matter where you are in the world, it is easiest to make money off women and children. The intuition, though some may claim overly stereotypical, has proven to be very much true, as both women and children seem to "significantly" reduce the level of their rationality the minute they step into a shopping mall. When it comes to kids and their shopping needs, they no doubt will turn to their parents to convince them to purchase. On the other hand, parents would usually like to satisfy their kids' requests as far as their budget is allowed, because they would feel happy when they see their children happy. Most likely, it is this psychology that helps give rise to a gigantic toy industry in the past decades.

In 2005, worldwide toys sales amounted to USD $63.7 billion, and the average annual growth rate at the time was approximately 5 % a year. About 5 years later, in 2010, these sales managed to maintain pretty much the same growth pace, but the sheer volume of the industry had reached $83.3 billion, according to a report released by the NPD Group in France.[1] As a result of the financial crisis, toys sales in Europe and the US showed some downward trends in these years. At the same time, however, the Asia market rose up to become the main impetus in pushing the toy market forward, with an annual growth rate as high as 9.2 % in the years around 2010. A more detailed geographical distribution of toy consumption can be observed from the following chart:

[1] NPD Group, 'Brief Introduction of Global Toy Market', www.npd.com

[2] Toy Industry Association, www.toyassociation.org

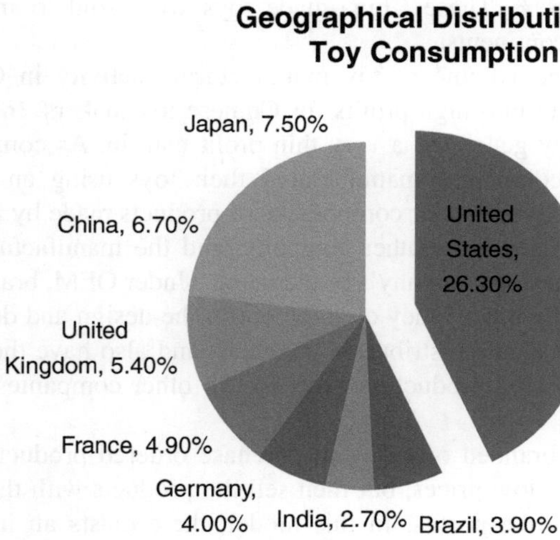


*Source* American Toy Industry Association[2]

Without question, the US is still the largest market for toys, making up over 26 % of worldwide toy consumption. They are followed by Japan with its 7.5 % share, and then China at 6.7 %. All other major toys consumption countries such as the UK (5.4 %), France (4.9 %), Germany (4.0 %), Brazil (3.9 %), and India (2.7 %), have less than 6 % share each of worldwide consumption. Therefore, a natural question is, for such a big pie with over $80 billion in value per year, who took away the largest piece of the pie in terms of profit?

China may be considered the "default" candidate for the taker of the largest piece of pie, as "Made in China" was printed on almost every single label of every toy sold in the world. There was a wide spread joke in China around 2010, citing a Chinese journalist who went to South Africa to cover the World Cup, and wanted to bring back World Cup souvenirs for his friends and colleagues back home. But he encountered an unexpected problem at the souvenir shop in South Africa—all the souvenirs were marked "Made in China", and, in fact, the manufacturing plant was in a location not far away from his hometown. The journalist worried that if he brought these gifts back, his friends and colleagues would suspect that he had bought them at the local stands near his home.

The joke reflects the reality that most of the toys in today's global toy market were, in fact, manufactured in China. As statistics reveal,[3] about half of the toys sold in the world were manufactured in China in early 2002, and this number continued to rise in subsequent years. In 2008, toys had become one of the five pillar products of export for China, and the proportion of the worldwide toys made

---

2 Toy Industry Association, www.toyassociation.org

3 Initial Public Offering Prospectus of Alpha Animation.

in China reached 75 %. These China-made toys were sold to more than 100 countries across all continents.

However, the large volume of toy manufacturing activity in China did not automatically translate into high profits for Chinese toy makers. In fact, the Chinese toy industry only generated a very thin profit margin. As common practice, most Chinese toys companies manufactured their toys using an OEM model. Under this model, the products or components of products made by manufacturing companies are purchased by another company, and the manufacturer's products retail under the purchasing company's brand name. Under OEM, brand owners can leverage the core technologies they own to control the design and development of new products as well as the distribution channels, and also have the flexibility of outsourcing some specific production processes to other companies through contracts and orders.

Under OEM, the branded owners can purchase ordered products from manufacturers at extremely low prices, but then sell the products with their own brand names at very handsome profits. In this model, there exists an inherently high degree of product homogeneity, which results in fierce competition for the manufacturers, but strong brand recognition and solid positioning for the product designers. The phrase "one high and three lows" was used to describe China's toy industry: a high-volume of exported toys but low technology content, low added value to brand, and low economic benefits. For example, under the OEM model, if the US retail price of a toy is $50, the Chinese toy manufacturer usually only captures a trivial piece of that revenue at about $1.[4]

As can be expected, manufacturers in this position on the supply chain are extremely vulnerable to risks. So it isn't surprising that when the 2008 financial crisis broke out, many OEM companies in China were among the first group of Chinese companies to close shop. As a consequence of these closures and the shrinking of foreign toy orders, the surviving Chinese toy companies had to find a new way to survive and grow. In this situation, many of Chinese toy makers reoriented their focus to China's domestic market, and began to explore the origination of their own branded products. Alpha Animation is one of the top representative cases in this effort.

## 8.2 An Underdeveloped Domestic Market

If turning to China's domestic market, what are the state, structure, and status of China's toy industry in the last decade? As previously mentioned, China, the "world's toy factory," houses a large number of toy manufacturing companies. These companies are highly clustered around several coastal areas, such as Guangdong, Jiangsu, Zhejiang, Shandong and Shanghai, which are also among the

[4] http://www.eeo.com.cn/eeo/jjgcb/2010/06/21/173106.shtml

most developed regions in China and the earliest to open up to foreign markets. By the end of February 2008, the number of large and medium-sized toy manufacturers in these five areas alone accounted for 88 % of the total companies in the Chinese toy industry, and contributed to more than 95 % of China's annual toy sales.[5] Among the five, Guangdong is the largest manufacturing and export region in all of China, and also the home of Alpha Animation.

As an export oriented industry, the Chinese toy industry ended up selling most of its products abroad, and these foreign companies took approximately 80 % of the value created by China's toy sales. Also, compared with the 150,000 categories of toys in the world, only about 30,000 are sold in China's domestic market. However, the demand for toys in China's still has great augmentation potential. A survey[6] shows that, compared with $288 in Japan, $290 in US, $323 in UK, and $34 on average in the world, the toy consumption of Chinese children per capita is only about $10. It significantly lags behind the demand in developed countries by a large gap. If we used the world consumption average as a benchmark, the consumption of toys by the 265 million Chinese children should be about $9 billion; in reality, it is only $4.2 billion. There exists a gap of $5.7 billion.

More importantly, toys are not only for children. They are for adult as well. In the US, more than 40 % of all animated figures are specially designed and produced for adults. In Japan, adult animated figures take up a 65 % share of the entire toys market. Among Japanese adults who are over 18 years old, at least 84 % of them own animated figures. In China, the demand for such adult-oriented toys is also very large. According to a survey conducted by Social Survey Institute of China,[7] 64 % of adult consumers say that they will consider buying animated figures if their financial condition allows. Among them, 33 % adults say they "like and are willing to buy toys."Since the purchasing power is higher for adults than for children, adults are often willing to spend more discretionary income on toys they may like. Over time, such market potential in the adult sector has caught the interest of toy makers such as Alpha Animation, and will assume a role in shaping the future of toy production in China.

## 8.3 Animated Toys: A Path to Transformation

So the question remains -what must Chinese toy makers like Alpha do to bridge the apparent gap between high domestic market potential and lackluster profitability? After years of exploration, Alpha selected animated toys as the route for change and success. As commonly defined, animated toys are toys that are

[5] National Bureau of Statistic of China, http://www.stats.gov.cn/

[6] NPD Group, 'Toy Industry, Opportunity Stand with Challenge', https://www.npd.com

[7] Social Survey Institute of China, http://www.chinasurvey.com.cn/

designed based on the figures and characters in animated movies. Think Spider-man or Batman.

It seemed to Alpha that animation possessed both important social values and significant financial value. From a sociological perspective, animated figures are carriers of the culture of a nation, and influence the people in an easily digestible and light-hearted way. People easily remember the stories behind animated figures. From a financial perspective, animation generates a whole chain of supply around the creation of a single animated character, since animation takes many forms—movies, books, toys, stationery, etc. In addition, animation is not a one-time "disposable" product. It is dynamic, and can be consumed recurrently. For example, let's take Barbie. Even though it is not animated in film, Barbie has all her own clothing line, jewelry collection, and dollhouse. She even has a boyfriend, who was drawn from her life stories. Mattel Inc., the firm that produces Barbie, produced different kinds of Barbie in accordance with different cultures and different time period, so as to capture the eyes and hearts of girls from all different countries. As a result, Barbie sold well for many decades, accompanying generations of young girls and creating generous long-term profits for the brand.

In China, in order for any business to be successful, it needs the blessing of government policies, which in many cases is simply a matter of good timing. It just so happened that in 2008, China announced new policies to support the development of the domestic animation industry by requiring every television station to add a channel for domestic animated movies while simultaneously restricting the showing of foreign ones.[8] This policy helped create an immediate open market for animation, and stimulated a rapid growth of Chinese domestic animated movie production. In recent years, domestic animated movies have increased at an annual growth rate of over 30 %. Taking TV animation shows as an example, only 4 series were produced nation wide in 1993, with a running time of 195 min in all, according to China's State Administration of Radio, Film and Television. In 2001, however, the number of series jumped to 13, with a total running time of 8,511 min. In 2008, 249 domestic animation TV series were created, spiking the total running time of animated TV to 131,042 min.[9]

As a toy maker facing the challenges of a transitioning industry, Alpha quickly identified and caught this window opportunity, which is to say, it decided to expand from a pure toy manufacturer who only manufactured the animated figures designed by big global brands to a designer of its own figures. It moved from only making toys to also making animated movies with its own specially branded animated figures. Apparently, this business model developed by Alpha required a much higher-level use of capital, the ability to create originally, and the capability to combine toys and animated movies. On the other hand, however, since popular

[8] The State Administration of Radio Film and Television, 'Policies for Promoting Development of the Domestic Animation Industry', www.gov.cn/gzdt/2008-08/19/content_1075077.htm

[9] The State Administration of Radio Film and Television, http://www.sarft.gov.cn/

animated figures are scarce resources, success in using this model would bring much higher returns than average.

## 8.4 Alpha's Road to the Top

Alpha started its transition by working with TV stations in China. In addition to continuing to manufacture traditional toys, Alpha also bought the rights to broadcast foreign animation movies in many cities in China. In this way, Alpha not only started to build up its own name as an authorized agent of these famous foreign animations, but they also established cooperative relationships with major TV stations. This laid an important foundation for Alpha, allowing the firm to show its own animated movies in the future. As an example, the popular animation "Pokemon" was brought to China by Alpha; as a matter of fact, it was also the company's "first touch" with animated toys.

In 2004, as part of its development strategy, Alpha Animation determined to pave a new path to integrate animated movies and animated toys. As an inexperienced explorer, Alpha adopted a parallel approach in order to mitigate the risks. On one hand, it enhanced its collaboration with famous foreign animation companies, such as Bandai Co. of Japan to obtain an authorization to produce and sell their well-known animated figures such as Ultraman, an animated figure adored by young boys in Asia. Through the partnership, Alpha gained some desperately needed experience in the animations industry.

At the same time, Alpha started exploration in designing and creating its own animated figures, such as Firepower Teenager King 1. As a traditional toys manufacturer, designing their own animated figures represented their penetration into the upstream sector of the toy industry value chain. Alpha promoted its own animated figures both on-line and off-line. While the corresponding animated movies were showing on TV channels, Alpha held road shows for its newly created toy figures in large toy stores across all of China's biggest cities. They even organized contests based on these newly created animated stories to generate buzz and encourage active consumer participation. In a relatively short period of time, Alpha created an entire sequence of popular animated figures such as Warrior Armor and the Little Witch, and took leadership of China's animated toy market.

## 8.5 The Secret of Alpha's Success

In a competitive market, profitability typically comes from a company's ability to find a unique, successful business model. As an industry leader, what actually made Alpha stand out? As will be discussed, Alpha's business model possesses several distinct features, allowing it to distinguish it from both domestic and foreign competitors.

### 8.5.1 Horizontal Cross-Media Integration

One notable feature of Alpha's business model is the horizontal integration of animated toys with animated movies; in other words, an integration across media. In the animation market, there were several ways by which animation companies could develop their businesses. The first one is through the development and licensing of animated movies and videos, as adapted by companies such as Disney. Disney created numerous animated figures, and, through licensing agreements, was able to show movies containing these animated figures around the world. In 2008, revenue from licensing took about 53 % of Disney's total revenue from animation-related products.[10] Another commonly used technique is through the development of animated toys, as represented by the companies such as Hasbro from the US and Bandai of Japan. The choice of company's development made by these companies pretty much reflected each company's unique set of strengths and weaknesses.

Alpha Animation, as a traditional toy manufacturer, certainly had tremendous experience in toys manufacturing. However, from a product promotion perspective, animated movies and videos were a much faster and more efficient way to go. Therefore, Alpha Animation carefully selected combination of animated toys and animated movies as its double-core business. Under this model, Alpha first designed its own animated figures, then made its own animated movies with these Alpha-created figures, and showed them nationwide. Meanwhile, it also manufactured toys along with these animated figures that were also sold nationwide. Using this strategy, the movies and videos could be considered advertisement for the toys, and, in turn, the toys would perpetuate consumer interest after the movies were over. Also, compared to the traditional toys makers, Alpha's toys, in general, possessed more cultural content and were backed by much stronger marketing support such as TV shows. The synergy from all these factors inevitably increased the profit margin of the toys that were sold. On the other hand, on the film side, compared to pure content creation firms, Alpha's toys sales helped financially support the early fund investment needed to create these animated figures.

[10] United Security, "From Producer to Industry Pioneer": www.lhzq.com

### 8.5.2 Sticking with Big Names

Another interesting feature of Alpha's unique business model is its co-development alongside already well-established global brands, such as Hasbro of US and Bandai of Japan, sharing in the reputation, experience, capacity and sales channels of the big names. For a recent example, Alpha Animation signed a long-term co-development contract in 2013 with Hasbro to establish a joint venture, which plans to focus on animated toys and related products, distribution, and providing authorized sales on a global scale. With this joint venture, Alpha obtained a shortcut to the vast foreign markets by joining hands with Hasbro. So far, the revenue generated from authorized sales of famous foreign brands accounts for 10 % of the Alpha's total revenue each year.[11]

### 8.5.3 Vertical Integration of Sales Channels

Alpha's third distinct feature is its wide and deep level of collaboration with its sales channels. Alpha adopts a Three-tier sales channel approach covering from dealers to distributors to retailers, as illustrated by the following diagram:

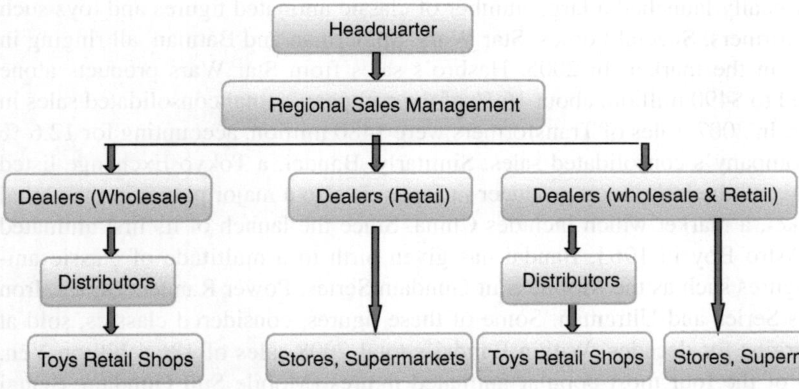


Alpha planted seeds early when it came to building its sales channels nationwide. After years, Alpha has setup stable long-run sales relationships with 137 regional dealers throughout China, and its products are sold in over 13,000 department stores, supermarkets and toy retail shops all over the country. Through these channels, Alpha's new products can be instantly shipped from manufacturing to the outlets nearest to the necessary consumers.

[11] All data of Alpha are from the Prospectus of Alpha unless indicated otherwise.

In addition, Alpha also established partnerships with TV stations on a long-term basis, encouraging in-depth cooperation through sponsoring TV program contests and other animated movie related activities. Under its agreement with TV stations, Alpha provides free animated movies to TV stations and, in turn, receives the primary right to primetime slots on popular channels. Meanwhile, Alpha also paid cooperation fees, which are generally low, to TV stations, for the opportunity to jointly organize TV program contests and free news coverage of Alpha's products. By 2008, Alpha's animation works were shown in 29 out of China's 31 provinces, broadcasting on 145 TV channels with an accumulated running time of 541,500 min. Between January and June of 2009, Alpha's animation works were further expanded to all 31 provinces on over 200 TV channels with a total running time of 291,500 min; this progress occurred in just a half-year span. Certain traditional media outlets such as Juvenile King of Comics magazines also published Alpha's animations. In 2010, Alpha even acquired 60 % of equity in JIAJIA Television, signaling that it has started to build up its own downstream sales channels.

This strong sales-channel-backed business model helped Alpha gain significantly competitive advantages over its more famous and formidable foreign competitors, such as Hasbro of the US and Bandai of Japan. In order to get a sense of the scale of Alpha's competitors, let's take a quick look at Hasbro, which is listed in NYSE, and one of the world's largest toy companies. Since the 1980s, it has continually launched a large number of classic animated figures and toys such as Transformers, Special Forces, Star Wars, Spiderman and Batman, all ringing in hot sales in the market. In 2005, Hasbro's sales from Star Wars products alone amounted to $490 million, about 16 % of the company's total consolidated sales in that year. In 2007, sales of Transformers were $480 million, accounting for 12.6 % of the company's consolidated sales. Similarly, Bandai, a Tokyo Exchange listed company and the largest toy producer in Japan, is also a major player in the global toy market, a market which includes China. Since the launch of its first animated figure, Astro Boy in 1963, Bandai has given birth to a multitude of classic animated figures such as the Mobile Suit Gundam Series, Power Rangers Series, Iron Warriors Series and Ultraman. Some of these figures, considered classics, sold at high margins for decades. Within Bandai's total 2008 sales of 126.4 billion Yen, the sum of the four most popular animated figures (Mobile Suit Gundam, Sentai Series, Dragon Ball and Masked Rider) contributed to 22.19 %.[12]

Both Hasbro and Bandai took an authorized sales approach by utilizing an agency to sell their products in China. However, these authorized agencies, except for Alpha, were in no way as strong of sales channels as were Alpha's, whose long-term contracts and mutually beneficial relationships encouraged loyalty and diligence from their domestic sales channel partners. As a result, even though both Hasbro and Bandai may be considered more "famous" brands globally, in China's toy market, they are not the best sellers. China's best toy seller is, hands down,

---

[12] Mingsheng Security, "China's Hasbro, A Future Leader: www.mszq.com

Alpha Animation.[13] The horizontal integration strategy backed by its well-developed sales channels won Alpha Animation its position at the top of China's toy market.

### *8.5.4 Competing on Branding, Not Pricing*

Another critical aspect of Alpha's business model is a strong branding effort, which they adopted against domestic competitors such as Dongguan Silverlit Toys Manufactory, Ltd. and Huan Qi Plastic Toys, Ltd. In contrast with a traditional strategy of competing on low pricing, as was typical for many "Made in China" companies, Alpha Animation focused on brand building at a very early stage in its corporate development. In particular, with the strong presence of the global big names such as Hasbro, Mattel and Bandai in China, still competing on low pricing can only drive Alpha to a low-end niche market.

There were several milestones in Alpha's brand-building journey. In 2001, one of Alpha's key products, "AULDEY with Double Diamonds," was named "Excellent Brand of Children's Products in China" by the editorial board of a well-watched event, called "Satisfied Consumption in Beijing."The news was then relayed on People's Daily, the largest newspaper in China. In January of 2005, Alpha was ranked 20th on the list of "China's Top 100 Potentials 2005" by Forbes Magazine. Also in 2005, Alpha became the first company in the toy industry to be accredited by China's State Administration for Industry and Commerce as a "Famous Trademark of China", and its "AULDEY with double diamonds" electric toys were awarded a "Famous Brand of China". In 2008, the "AULDEY" brand that Alpha Animation had cultivated and nurtured for over a decade was accredited as a "Famous Trademark of China," "Famous Brand of China," and made the list of China's Top Ten Toy Brands 2008.

### *8.5.5 Innovation as the Bottom Line*

The last remarkable feature that makes Alpha's business model unique among Chinese toy makers is its continued effort in building up independent Innovation capacity. All brands are more or less defined by the owner company's capacity of innovation, regardless it be an innovation of design, manufacturing, packaging, processing, or marketing. No innovation, no branding. In China's toy market, Alpha has been considered the most "innovative" Chinese company. From 2006 to 2009, the patents that Alpha obtained in China exceeded 100 each year, and all of them were commercialized immediately. The number of intellectual properties that

[13] Guangdong Toy Association, http://gdta.ctoy.com.cn/

Alpha owns ranks first in the all of China’s toy industry as well, and Alpha independently developed, produced and sold over 100 SKUs each year. Alpha is the industry leader in terms of the product design, production technology and external packaging.

Since 2007, Alpha’s original animation creation has sped up as well. At present, Alpha possesses the production capacity to create almost 5,000 min of animated movies, and its ongoing production of films has already reached about 7,300 min. Alpha’s original animation is also heading towards a much more diverse set of audiences: the co-development of children movies and movies for older audiences; the joint launching of animated pieces and live action films; the combination of domestic and foreign animated figures, featuring original and non-original animated figures.

It is all these distinct characteristics of Alpha’s business model that allows it such a unique competitive advantage in the market, helping transform Alpha from a typical “Made in China” firm to a differentiated “Designed in China” company. This difference not only catapulted Alpha to the top of its industry, it also made them a role model for many Chinese companies to follow in the post-financial crisis era, as Chinese companies across the map are readjusting their business models for more sustainable long-term growth.

## 8.6 Can’t Make it Without Investors, and So Make it for Investors

The maximization of shareholders’ wealth is always an inevitable goal of any company, regardless it be a private firm or a public entity. This goal is also why business models are developed in the first place; it becomes a virtuous cycle. Successful business models, needless to say, bolster the firm with more promising cash flows and more mitigated risk. In turn, the capital inflow subsequently provides the firm with needed funds to support the development and implementation of its business model. Alpha’s success in listing on the Chinese capital market is a quintessential example of the positive interaction between a successful business model and external financing, and between the product market and the financial market.

Since its inception, Alpha Animation has financed with capital three times, and conducted three times of equity transfer. These financing activities provided Alpha with adequate cash to implement its ambitious business plans, including its horizontal cross-media integration, talent recruiting, R&D for original design and the creation of its own animated figures, development of its three-tier sales channels, licensing fees on figures by global brands, and finally its brand building. The successful implementation of these business plans, in turn, also helped Alpha generate very appealing financial statements.

As estimated by United Securities,[14] the sales of animated toys independently designed by Alpha from 2009 to 2011 grew by 91, 13.5 and 22.7 % each year, respectively, and Alpha's authorized sales of animated toys designed by global brands also maintained a steady growth rate of 15 %. These stable increases in the sales revenue provided solid returns for equity investors. From 2009 to 2011, Alpha achieved earning per share (EPS) at 0.65 RMB, 0.85 RMB and 1.10 RMB, respectively, signaling growth of 59, 31 and 30 % each year. It came of no surprise, then, that Alpha Animation successfully listed on the Shenzhen Stock Exchange on August 10th, 2009.

Before the IPO, Alpha had three owners—CaiXiaodong (17 %), CaiDongqing (68 %), and Li liqing (15 %). After the IPO, about 25 % of shares were released to the general public, and the three previous shareholders CaiXiaodong (12.75 %), CaiDongqing (51 %), and Li liqing (11.25 %) jointly maintained 75 % of the shares of the firm.

With its IPO, Alpha Animation issued 40 million shares at a price of 22.92 RMB per share. Totally, it raised about 900 million RMB, which provided a new source of equity capital to support Alpha's continued transformation into "Designed in China", sustaining Alpha's growth for years to come.

---

14 United Securities, 'From Producer towards Leaders of the Industry', www.lhzq.com

# Chapter 9
# China's Warner Brothers: The Story of Huayi Brothers Media

**Abstract** Until the beginning of this century, China's film market had been monopolized by a few state-owned film makers. Even though privately-held movie companies are now allowed to produce movies thanks to the slight de-regulatory rules of the last decade, government clout over the industry is still strong. However, Huayi Brothers, a leading privately-held movie maker whose case will be discussed in this chapter, performed remarkably well despite this heavily regulated market environment by creating a unique business development model.

**Keywords** Film industry · Government regulation · Privately-owned filmmakers · Double cores · Triple play

In these days in China, it would be considered outdated if the only filmmakers that come to mind are a few state-owned ones. In particular, a filmmaker called Huayi Brothers Media Corporation, a privately-owned company established in 2000 and a standout among consumers and investors has become a rising star in past years. In these days, audiences instinctively raise their expectations for a film if they see Huayi listed as the producer. So, of course, the question of interest is—how did Huayi become a leading film company in just 9 years? How did they manage to successfully list in the stock market? And most importantly, what is Huayi's secret for surpassing all its competitors? For finding the answers for all these questions, let's take a closer look at this company in this chapter.

## 9.1 China's Film Industry in Past Decades

To fully understand China's film industry, we have to familiarize ourselves first with the role played by the Chinese government. In the 1990s, state-owned film makers monopolized the film industry, primarily because the government wanted strict control over the theme and content of all films. In some senses, this effect is still present today. Most film studios, even private ones, are coerced into occasionally producing some "mainstream" films to satisfy government need. There came a seemingly flourishing prospect for private filmmakers, however, as the new century



J. G. Wang and J. Yang, *Who Gets Funds from China's Capital Market?*,
SpringerBriefs in Business, DOI: 10.1007/978-3-642-44913-0_9, 

dawned: the government relaxed certain regulations. Some state-owned film studio underwent reforms allowing a few private filmmakers to come into being.

To be certain, government regulation, in general, remained considerably strict, and the barrier to entry remained high. Films were to be inspected strictly, even for those with a license (or permission to access), and the inspection was even tighter for the imported films. Such regulation has restricted the development of the Chinese film industry to some degree. On top of that, the high cost of film production resulted in new forms of filmmaking entities—film studios that could only produce low cost short films. The cost and box office returns of such films were typically limited to several million RMB. Previously developed state owned film studios had already grabbed the majority of the resources for film production, creating an oligopoly in China's film industry and leaving limited resources for smaller competing firms. A parallel can be drawn from this to the situation in Hollywood when the Hays Code was issued in 1935 and the Paramount decision was carried out in 1948.

## 9.2 Who Owns the Box Office?

When it comes to sales, the Chinese film industry has changed and developed greatly since the arrival of the twenty-first century. Annual box office sales fell below RMB 1 billion in 1995 with less than 100 films being produced that year. In the new century, however (take 2006 as an example), the box office sales were RMB 2.62 billion, almost doubled from 11 years ago. 2006 also witnessed the fourth consecutive annual increase of box office sales.[1] The following graph can illustrate this trend further:

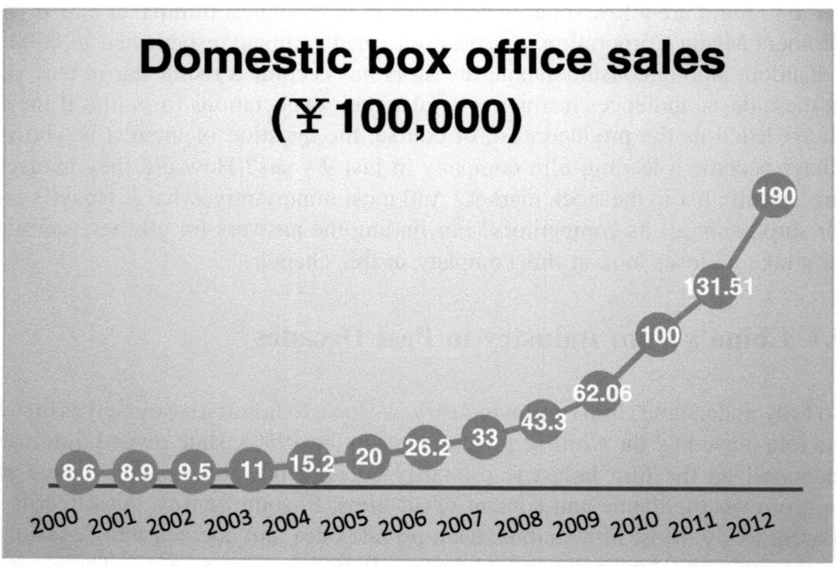


[1] Annual Domestic Box Office Sales, The State Administration of Radio Film and Television, http://www.sarft.gov.cn/

There has been a historical shortage of high quality film in China. The top three winners in Chinese box office history—Avatar, Transformers, and the Titanic—are all made overseas. Among the top ten, only five are domestically produced. One reason for this is simply that domestic investment into creative talent and execution is overwhelmingly lower than the amount invested in most foreign countries.

Blockbusters that impress with splendid spectacles, fancy special effect, all-star casts, and good box office records require big investments, and the funding for films in China had been insufficient until 2008. In 2008, according to data from the State Administration of Radio Film and Television, China's film industry recorded historically high numbers, with eight domestically produced films achieving over 100 million RMB each in box office sales. This number exceeded the total number in both 2006 and 2007 combined that managed to earn more than 100 million RMB. Also in 2008, eight domestic films entered into the top 10 of China's film rankings and took over the top five in box office rankings. The increase of the high quality film in both content and execution shot up market demand and enhanced the comparative advantage of domestic producers.

Several big film companies control China's film industry, as illustrated by the market shares in the Table 9.1.

China Film Group is the leading company in the market. Its film production in the last 3 years account for 12 % of the entire market and its films—with its 100 million plus sales—make up 31 % of the sales of films in the same category.[2] In other words, China Film Group is first in terms of film releasing, box office sales and market share. But this success is indubitably a result of its state ownership status and the resulting monopoly advantages it is able to gain. For example, one of its subsidiaries—the movie channel program production center CCTV-6—is the only film channel on TV authorized by the government. Such advantage is beyond the reach of any privately owned film producers.

It is therefore impressive that of the top seven, three are privately-owned filmmakers: Huayi Brothers, Bona Film Group Limited (the first one to obtain a Film Distribution License from the government) and Beijing New Pictures Co., Ltd. Among these, Huayi Brothers tops the chart.

## 9.3 Huayi's Core Businesses

Huayi was founded by two brothers, Zhongjun Wang and Zhonglei Wang in 1994. The word "Brothers" was added to the company name not only because it was founded by two brothers, but also as a sign of respect and aspiration to Warner Brothers in hopes of someday becoming the Chinese counterpart of the famed American filmmaker. The main businesses of Huayi consist of film production, TV

2 *'2007 Chinese Film Industry Report'*, China Film Association, China Film Press.

show production and talent agency functions. Its main revenue comes from the box office, cashing in on broadcast rights, advertising revenue, audio–video product royalties, and commission from its talent agency segment. Some well-known films produced by Huayi include Painted Skin, If You Are The One, Project BB and Kung Fu.

Huayi started from scratch in the pure play film-making industry, but truly thrived after entering the TV series industry. Huayi produced on average three to four films per year before 2009, two of which received lofty investments and became incredibly popular, ushering in subsequently high box office sales. The films produced all became popular films with high commercial value and good box office figures. Huayi can also produce an average of about 300 episodes of TV each year. Take Soldiers Sortie for example—it was the top TV show of its year, and also won the title for best director in the Golden Eagle Awards in China. The TV series business, which makes up 55.23 % of the firm's total revenue, has become the pillar of the company.[3]

Huayi faces intense competition specifically from state-owned companies such as Beijing Hairun Film Group and China Central Television, the latter of which is actually the top state-owned company in the entertainment industry and possesses enormous resources and capital.

## 9.4 What Is Behind Huayi's Success?

Huayi stays competitive in this environment by fine-tuning its core competencies and understanding the value it offers in the market. Huayi's core competences include the following:

### *9.4.1 Celebrities as Shareholders*

By examining the list of Huayi's top shareholders, we can find many shining stars—literally. Numerous celebrities and A-listers make up the list of Huayi's main investors. Let us pick Jack Ma, Xiaogang Feng, Jizhong Zhang and Xiaoming Huang as just four examples, these four are truly indicative of Huayi's strategic position in the market as they all play different roles in the film industry and made different contributions to the company.

Jack Ma, the CEO of Alibaba, is one of the most famous entrepreneurs in China, one with great vision, courage and insight for business. One of his primary business lines is Taobao, the largest personal auction website in Asia. He became

[3] All data of Huayi Brothers are from Initial Public Offering Prospectus of Huayi Brothers unless indicated otherwise.

the shareholder of Huayi for two reasons: first, he believed in the great growth potential of the film industry; second, he valued the business model adopted by Huayi as he is a good friend of Huayi's owner Zhongjun Wang and knows the company well. But how important exactly is Jack Ma's investment to Huayi? First and most obviously, it was important because Jack Ma brought equity capital that Huayi needed, obtaining 10.7 % of the shares of Huayi through a share transfer in 2006. The injection of capital for filmmaking companies starts a virtuous cycle—sufficient capital guarantees a smooth production process for the film; a good quality product can in turn earn a better box office and the company, therefore, can take a larger market share to create more quality films. However, Jack Ma's positive influence as Huayi's investor extended beyond just the money—in a domino effect, Jack Ma also encouraged many of his successful friends to invest in Huayi as well. The CEO of Focus Media, for example, followed Jack Ma in becoming a shareholder in 2008. In a fame-crazed Chinese entertainment industry, the power a world famous entrepreneur possesses should not be underestimated in his ability to make investors confident about Huayi.

While on the topic of influential entrepreneurs, it should be noted that the personal charisma of Huayi's founder Zhongjun Wang in attracting and influencing potential investors was also indispensable to the success of the company. Because of his personable nature and ease of business dealings, Huayi was able to gain a comparative advantage that could not easily be replicated by competitors in a short period of time.

### *9.4.2 Double Core Competencies: Production and Talent*

Next, let us turn to the three other big shots who contributed greatly to determining the success of Huayi—Xiaogang Feng, Jizhong Zhang and Xiaoming Huang. Together they reflect the uniqueness of the business model Huayi developed and they are also Huayi's core talent pool. Xiaogang Feng is a famous movie director, Jizhong Zhang is a well-known play writer, and Xiaoming Huang is a famous actor. They play different roles in the film production process, and Huayi integrated them brilliantly into a genius filmmaking team. This is truly the most special part of Huayi's model: Huayi integrated its talent agency business with its film business, while at the same time allowing the talent agency business to also serve the two other major businesses of Huayi—the film and TV businesses—creating a synergy among the three segments.

For their part, the film and TV businesses provide precious opportunity for the performers and ensure the smooth operation of the talent agency business. Conversely, the abundant talent pool provides a steady supply of outstanding cast members for the various films and shows, lowering operation costs and guaranteeing quality of Huayi's final products.

This synergy was evident in the first film that Huayi produced, a movie called "Endless" that was directed by Xiaogang Feng. At that time, Xiaogang's box office record wasn't that strong, but his films had a special style that Huayi noticed immediately. Zhongjun Wang hired Xiaogang Feng and then started to build the Feng Brand. Huayi managed to merge Xiaogang's fame for creating extraordinary products with Huayi's own branding, enhancing both in the process.

This also demonstrated the successful talent training system that Huayi had in place. At the beginning, Xiaogang Feng mainly produced comedies. Although his films were of high quality, the genre itself restricted his pieces from gaining high box office recognition; in other words, the films needed more commercialization. In addition, Xiaogang Feng focused only on year-end holiday movies and ignored the overseas market. Huayi, after hiring Feng, picked up some specific film themes for him according to his unique style, but also tailored to market demand. These themes included war, costume movies and many other more complex and profound themes that Feng now created in addition to year-end holiday movies. Thanks to the effort, Xiaogang Feng became one of the most famous directors in China's film society and earned box office sales on par with those of Yimou Zhang and Kaige Chen, the two most famous movie directors in China.

Xiaogang Feng is only the beginning of the directing talent that Huayi nurtured. Many other new directors such as Chuan Lu, Shuzi Lin, Ershan Wu, Delun Feng and Haoxiang Peng, all of whom were just starting out in their various genres, were scouted by Huayi and made into success stories. This "diversification" brought more creativity to the film production and also tied the brand "Huayi" with big names. Of course, Huayi has to sell some big shares to Xiaogang Feng in 2007 in order to retain such a talent.

Before talking about another one of Huayi's major talents, Jizhong Zhang, it's important to first understand the role of a producer in the film production process. If a script is a roughcast house, then the directors and cast members are the ones who furnish the house, and the producer is the one who connects these different elements into a synchronized entity. The most important task for the producer is finding the best script. Let's take a look at the extent of the "star effect" that famous producers brought to Huayi.

The owner of Huayi, Junzhong Wang, once commented that a talented producer is the scarcest of all scarce resources. His brother Zhonglei Wang specifically lauded Jizhong Zhang as one such producer because of the audience loyalty and international fame of his ancient customs TV series. For Chinese TV program developers, especially those who produce family or drama shows, there is a constant struggle to translate domestic popularity into international popularity and sales, but Zhang's costume-sword-play dramas sold exceptionally well both in and outside China, especially, in other Asian countries. In turn, Huayi created a very favorable working environment for Zhang. Zhang's team only takes charge of creativity and production while the other issues such as public relationship and advertising campaign are all taken care of by other departments in Huayi. The delegation of logistics to Huayi's execution teams allowed Jizhong Zhang to focus on his creative work and save him more time and energy to create better content. It is also one of Huayi's distinguishing features that Xiaoming Huang, a huge movie star in Chinese circuits, is among the firm's shareholders, and he is not alone.

Huayi has attracted numerous superstars, A-list celebrities as investors through the implementation of its exclusive agent system. This creates a symbiotic relationship between Huayi and the stars, guarantying high quality, star-studded casts for Huayi's films while simultaneously helping the stars establish their own brand and earn more box office revenue. The film 'The Equation of Love & Death,' to take just one example, was tailored specifically for Huayi agency actress Xun Zhou. Huayi has gathered a large number of movie stars through its talent agency process and the shares held by these stars increase their loyalty to the firm and encourage a sense of belonging. This business model significantly stabilized the talent agency business that Huayi created.

Combining this star power with the fact that excellent directors and performers are the scarcest of resources, thanks to their influence on market and box office tickets sales and ability to hike up the quality of films, Huayi's integration of top directors, producers and performers has resulted in a solid cycle of positive externalities. One plus one has become bigger than two.

### 9.4.3 Triple Play and Butterfly

Hauyi developed a triple-play business model they described as the "three linked major businesses," and having the characteristics of "industrialized operations". The three linked businesses are film, TV, and the talent agency business. The industry chain efficiently integrates all these resources, and Huayi took advantage of this to win the market, causing a simultaneous movement in the upstream and the downstream of the industry.

In the film business, theatres and cinemas lie at the downstream end of the industry. In china, films are slotted to show in cinemas or theatres after the production and inspection process. According to current regulations in China, production companies can only cooperate with theatre chains during the production process, and then the theatre chains will arrange and schedule showings in their various cinemas. The film production companies cannot directly sign contracts regarding showing schedule with individual cinemas, and have to cooperate with the middleman—the theatre chains. If we think of the production company as a food manufacturing plant, then the theatre chains would be supermarkets at which consumers can obtain the final goods.

Huayi has to negotiate with theatre chains for the scheduling of films and also for the division of box office earnings. Generally speaking, the theatre chain will take 40 % and the other 60 % belongs to the film studio. If a film producer has its own theater, however, then all the profit will go to the filmmaker itself. In addition, for filmmakers to own their own theatres shortens the distance between the consumer and the producer. This was the idea that Huayi had, but it was suspended until 2009, the year of its IPO, because of previously limited funding. As of 2012, Hauyi has invested in five theaters in five different cities. Huayi always holds premiers of their new films at these five theaters and invites stars to participate in promotional activities on site to generate buzz about their films and give Huayi a unique, experience-oriented edge over competitors. This set-up can effectively enhance Huayi's direct communication with audiences and works well to promote the brand of Hauyi. Vertical integration is helping Huayi grow into a diversified company with various business lines of film production, distribution, and screening, all in-house.

In addition to the vertical integration of talent agency business, film making business and theater chains, Huayi has also integrated its film and TV series businesses horizontally to create a "butterfly" shaped business model, one which has both vertical and horizontal integrations. Based on its success in the film industry, Huayi simply mimicked its movie business model in the TV series industry, where there are even more advantages for such a horizontal integration thanks to the synergy created by operating in film and TV simultaneously. First of all, the integration diversifies the operational risk of the whole company. The investment and risk on a single film is much larger than that of a long-running, multi-episode TV series; the combination of the two businesses can lower the overall portfolio operating cost. Second, the integration of film and TV enhances the brand competitiveness of the Huayi, giving it more visibility and volume to targeted consumer groups. Finally, the talent agency business can serve the film and TV businesses at the same time, killing two birds with one stone and maximizing synergy.

### 9.4.4 Winning Through Differentiation

As indicated in Table 9.1, Huayi is not the largest film maker in China in terms of revenue and market share, nor is it the only private film maker in the top-ten list of domestic film studios. And in addition to just domestic companies, Huayi also faces stiff competition from Hollywood films that are said to have "dominated" the Chinese market, taking the top three box office positions multiple years in a row.

It begs the question of how Huayi continues to be so successful in both generating brand integrity and generating revenue—the answer lies in differentiation. Let's take China Film Group—the leading film maker in China—and Bona Film Group Limited—another privately owned film maker—as comparisons.

China Film Group is a state owned enterprise, founded by the State Administration of Radio, Film and Television. Such a company has natural advantages since birth. Its monopoly power includes the exclusive right to import films and ownership of the only national film channel on Chinese TV. China Film Group also developed the complete-industry-chain model. Unlike Huayi and other privately held film makers, China Film Group has abundant capital, has full ownership over four theater chains and has partial ownership over others. This represents the most thorough industry integration in China's movie market today.

**Table 9.1** Market share of box office sales

| Box office rank | Company name | Number of top ten film | Total box office Sales | Proportion in the total box office of all the domestic films |
|---|---|---|---|---|
| 1 | China film group | 7.5 | 100,920 | 16.67 |
| 2 | Huayi Brothers media corporation | 7 | 92,570 | 15.57 |
| 3 | Shanghai film group | 5 | 56,200 | 9.45 |
| 4 | Bona film group limited | 7.5 | 32,540 | 5.47 |
| 5 | Beijing new pictures Co., Ltd | 1 | 23,000 | 3.87 |
| 6 | Edko film limited | 1 | 13,760 | 2.31 |
| 7 | Warner China film HG corporation | 1 | 2,300 | 0.39 |

*Data source* 2007 Chinese Film Industry Report, by China Film Association

For private companies like Huayi, China Film Group is (almost literally) the elephant in the room.

However, despite the pure volume that China Film Group possesses, Huayi manages to hold distinct advantages over them. China Film Group has not developed a talent agency business, and Huayi was able to capture that niche market. In addition, due to the nature of state-ownership and the requirements of the State Administration of Radio Film and Television, China Film Group is obligated under contract to frequently shoot films that promote government ideology or agenda, and this definitely leads to a decrease in commercial value of their brand.

Unlike the giant China Film Group, Bona Film Group Limited is also a privately held filmmaker with a core-competitiveness in film distribution. Bona has the authorization to distribute the films both domestically and internationally, and the films distributed are not restricted to theaters only; they also have the ability to distribute in other forms such as through DVDs, Blue-Ray Disc, and internet movie web portals such as Sina or Sohu. In addition, they have partnerships with AMCN, and TV channels to provide in-flight entertainment programs. However, comparing with Huayi, they were not well diversified in terms of their content and genre, and it took Bona a precious long time to realize the value of talent agency business, by which time Huayi had already gained valuable first-comer advantages and took the leading position among private filmmakers.

### *9.4.5 Industrializing Operations Management*

The presence of the foreign filmmakers in the Chinese film market has generated considerably competitive pressure for domestic players. But for the same token, it has also provided domestic filmmakers the opportunity to learn firsthand from their foreign counterparts, many of which are very successful. The industrialized operation system adopted by Huayi is exactly one such skill that was "imported" from foreign film companies. The key idea of this system is modulating the processes of all businesses and standardizing operations across these different businesses, giving the entire system as certain degree flexibility through financial management, organizational management, creativity management, marketing management and human resource management.

Standardized financial management can help to track the capital spending throughout a movie or TV shooting process, shortening the time span for accounts receivables and allowing the company to objectively evaluate the gap between actual sales and projected ones. In other words, standardized financial management focuses on performance assessment, budget control, and cash cycle, and can help those in management positions monitor the entire business operation process. It helped ensure the continued growth of Huayi's businesses.

The creativity management portion was based on a "Business Unit + Workshop" model which diversified the responsibilities of generating commercial value and those of creating artistry into different entities. The business unit was put in charge of maintaining the commercial value of films and the workshop unit was responsible for developing the artistry. The business unit provided capital and technical support to the workshop according to contracts so that the workshop is able to create content of the high quality in terms of artistry and creativity. The business unit also conducts periodical assessments for the workshops: if a piece from the workshop receives low box office sales, then subsequent capital support would be limited or cut off, and the contract could be terminated. This assessment process ensured that only the most successful products survive and go to market, maintaining the brand and integrity of the firm. In essence, the "Business Unit + Workshop" management model is a flexible system with division of labor, but under unified top-level management. The business unit manages the workshop to ensure quality while the workshop has the independence and autonomy to produce the artistry.

The marketing model that Huayi adopted includes the introduction of embedded ads and the development of movie-related derivatives, such as video/DVD, books, toys, web sites, games, souvenirs, apparels, and others. Embedded ads bring in ad income without causing negative consumer reaction as other intrusive advertising tends to do, and movie derivatives are already very popular in the foreign film industry and have long been used by foreign filmmakers. For example, the film derivatives of the "Star Wars", and "Harry Potter" all sold extremely well in China. These movie derivatives have been the cash cow of Huayi in recent years.

### 9.4.6 Going Far with Funding

No matter what ambitious plan a company may have and how well-designed their model is, if they don't have the fund to buy what they need to implement and execute, there plans remain, at best, just that—plans. Public listing, for any company, is always a milestone, representing a qualification the company possesses in order to be recognized by the general public and receiving those much needed funds to put those plans into action. However, an important insight that successful companies such as Huayi revealed is that this milestone can't be achieved without Pre-IPO financing.

Before their IPO, Huayi experienced three rounds of private equity (PE) financing. The first round of PE was launched in August 2000 when Taihe Holding Co. Ltd and Huayi each invested RMB 1.3 million and founded the Beijing Huayi Brothers Taihe Film Investment Co., Ltd. This joint venture laid down the foundation for their success in China's film industry in the following years. Later that year, Huayi acquired 40 % of the shares of Xian Movie Co. Ltd and renamed the newly acquired segment "Xiying Huayi," a segment that mainly focused on movies and television works. Huayi further increased its shares in Xiying Huayi in later years, and it eventually became the controlling shareholder.

The second round of PE was offered by Hong Kong TOM Group in late 2004. TOM Group invested USD $10 million in Huayi. Of that $10 million, $5 million was exchanged for 27 % of Huayi shares and the remaining $5 million was used to buy Huayi convertible bonds, which had an annual interest rate of 6 %. At the same time, Huayi sold 3 % of its shares to the China Equity Co., Ltd. at a price of USD $0.7 million. This round of PE raised the funds to a total of USD $10.7 million for the two owners, and their shares of company increased to 70 %.

The third round was to get Jack Ma into the play by allowing Jack Ma to purchase back the shares of Huayi from Taihe and TOM group and let the latter exit. Huayi launched a new round of private equity financing through Yahoo China, which was founded by Jack Ma. Due to the influence of Jack Ma, there came a wave of new investments in Huayi from various Zhejiang entrepreneurs.

During 2007 and 2008, many of Huayi's major shareholders began to transfer some of their shares to some staff and directors; they then further increased equity capital by issuing more new shares to the wide scope of employees and movie stars under Huayi.

Eventually, Huayi was ready to go public. In October 2009, Huayi Brothers was successfully listed in the Shenzhen Stock Exchange (Stock Ticker: 300027), raising RMB 12.0036 billion through the issuance of 42 million shares in the A share market at a price of RMB 28.58 per share. There were 168 million shares outstanding, and the earning per share (EPS) was RMB 2.22.[4]

---

[4] China IPO Consulting Net, '*A Case Study of Huayi Brother's IPO*', http://ipo.ocn.com.cn/info/201107/huayixiongdi271132.html

## 9.5 Looking Forward: Huayi's Rising Legacy

It is without question that the word to describe Huayi's outlook is "promising". When the path to public funding opened up, Huayi gained access to needed capital in a much wider scope. This sustainable funding will allow Huayi to expand its Butterfly model to a much wider scope as well. Huayi can use public equity to produce a larger volume of films and TV series to more aggressively gain market share. Meanwhile, Huayi can now spend more money on the recruitment of more top-of-the-industry directors and film producers to expand their portfolio of talent beyond just Xiaogang Feng and diversify its core technical team. Furthermore, Huayi continues to improve the quality and the commercial value of its existing performers and directors, enhancing the Huayi in the perception of consumers.

Thanks to the IPO, Huayi's vertical integration will be able go deeper as well. Huayi will be able to extend its theater chains to more cities in China to ensure better box office sales. In addition, Huayi is also ambitious in extending its brand name to the international market to get a larger slice of the big pie of overseas sales. With the money in hand, they are ready to go.

More than a century ago, when Warner brothers Harry, Albert, Sam and Jack opened their first theater in the town of New Castle in 1903, they never thought the business they created in the suburbs of Pennsylvania would one day become one of the largest entertainment empires in the world. They certainly didn't think, either, that their career would become the role model and inspiration for another pair of brothers on the other side of the Pacific Ocean 100 years later. With their success so far, the Huayi Brothers—Wang brothers by birth—are truly on their way to realizing their dream of becoming China's Warner Brothers someday, and analysts, investors, and audiences across China can't help but be inspired by the story and wish them luck. Hey, you never know!

# Chapter 10
# A Paver of the Road Not Taken: The Story of Huace Film and TV

**Abstract** Similarly to the movie industry, the TV series market in China is also strongly regulated by the government, and most of the dominant positions are still occupied by state-owned TV producers. Achieving success from the place of a niche player remains a great challenge, but Huace Film & TV, the leading privately-held TV series producer, demonstrated that it is a mission possible. This chapter will explore what Huace did and how it did it.

**Keywords** TV series · Culture market · New media · Script and scriptwriters · Positioning · Market channels

Culture is considered the newest industry that has been put on the list of government policy support in China and brought increased attention of the capital market. Among the companies involved in culture industry, the most notable ones should count these movie and TV series makers, including the company that we are going to talk about in this chapter. The company, called Zhejiang Huace Film and TV Co., Ltd., is one of the largest private TV series producers in China, and a company being listed in the Growth Enterprise Board of Shenzhen Stock Exchange (Ticker: 300133) in October 2010. The interest in this company lies in how Huace could timely caught this burgeoning opportunity and worked out its way to attract investors in public capital market, and what was the business model it developed to distinguish the firm from its competitors. Huace's case could also be a good window that helps better understand the fast growing culture market, in particular, the TV series industry in China.

## 10.1 A Rising Industry: From Exploration to Prosperity

The birth of the TV series in China, actually, could be traced back to 1958 when the first TV series was broadcasted. Even though it was born in 1958, however, the true start of the fast development of TV series, as an industry, in China should be

J. G. Wang and J. Yang, *Who Gets Funds from China's Capital Market?*,
SpringerBriefs in Business, DOI: 10.1007/978-3-642-44913-0_10, 

considered after 1978 when China began its reform and opening up to the rest of the world.

The China's TV series market experienced three-stages in its development in the past 30 years since 1978: exploration, growth and maturity. The exploration period was from 1978 to 1988 for about 10 years. During that period of time, national and local TV stations were the only TV series makers. Those TV stations, with reference on the TV series shown in Hong Kong, Taiwan and foreign countries, produced plays on variety of topics, such as family plays, war plays, action dramas, fiction dramas, crime dramas and others.

The growth period was from 1988 to 1998 for about another 10 years. During this period of time, more TV series varieties that cater to the audiences' preference were produced, and all types of plays such as the family plays, war plays, action dramas, fiction dramas, and crime dramas became more mature in this period of time. Some of them even made a sensation throughout the nation.

The maturity period is from 1998 until now. During this period time, more than 10,000 TV series were made every year. New varieties, such as the youth idol drama, science fiction and some others, started to emerge. What's worth special mentioning is that eight private television production companies obtained the A level license for TV production in 2008. In China, the A level license has always been an insurmountable barrier for private companies, and only the state owned TV stations and state owned TV and film companies were qualified to apply before 2008. Since 2008, however, government began to support the development of the private TV and film companies through some favorable policies. As a result, the market share of the private TV and film companies began to grow and kept an upward trend since then. Currently, there were more than 130 companies that received the A level license, among them, 1/3 are private companies. Meanwhile, with the opening up of the TV series market to private capital, especially after 2005 when the central government lifted the bar for private capital to enter into the culture industry, the TV series industry truly took off.

In some sense, the TV industry is closely linked with the political and cultural environment in China. In the early stage of the industry, the government positioned TV series purely as tools of propaganda. Later on, those TV series focusing on humanity were gradually developed and expanded, and human nature and human relationships were better displayed. In recent years, more materials were drawn from real life, and the figures displayed reflected wider variety of people from social elites, war heroes, to just some ordinary citizens. The contents also became more and more close-to-real-life, popular, secularizing and entertaining, reflecting the progress of China's culture system and environment.

Although the TV series industry was still regulated, the regulators have gradually permitted more makings of TV series opened up to all domestic companies including privately held firms. With relatively low threshold, and low market concentration, the TV series market can be considered, currently, a competitive one with many competitors. According to the data released from State Administration of Radio, Film and Television (SARFT), there are more than 130 companies that own the TV Series Production License (Class A), and 5,363 companies that have the Radio and Television Program Production and Operation Permit, and the number is still growing.[1] After 30 years, China has become the country with the largest number of TV series producers in the world.

There were 402 seasons of TV series (12,910 episodes) that obtained the domestic TV Series Production License and more than 4057 institutions being granted the Radio and Television Program Production and Operation Permit in 2009, and every television drama company has produced 0.1 season of TV series (3.18 episodes) on average. The market concentration, however, is low. For instance, those very famous TV series brands including Huace only have about 10 % market share.

### 10.1.1 Excess Supply and Growing Demand

The market for TV series in China has been characterized by excess supply for years. According to the data from the State Administration of Radio, Film and Television, there has been more than 20 % of TV series that were deserted due to either quality or theme issues. Based on a survey conducted by CSM[2] on TV series broadcast in 516 channels of 80 cities, only 412 TV series were broadcast in 2008 out of the 502 that have already obtained the homebred teleplay license issued in 2006.

Fortunately, however, the market demand kept growing. According to the data from SARFT, the total revenue of the National Broadcasting System reached 0.88 billion RMB in 1982 and 158.3 billion in 2008. The annual growth rate from 1982 to 2008 is more than 20 % on average, which is much higher than that of the national economy and has become an important emerging industry and the new growth spot. Up to today, China has significantly improved its broadcast capacity, coverage, and service quality by establishing a network with the largest coverage and multiple ways of transmission including wireless, cable, satellite, and internet, and parallel development of urban areas, rural areas, domestic market and international regions.

Recently, the price of TV series increased along with the improvement of its quality, and the total transaction volume continues to grow. In 2010, the total transaction hit 6 billion RMB with an increase of 8 % from the previous year. By August 2009, there were 277 TV stations, 0.4 billion TV sets and 0.163 billion cable TV subscribers, and the coverage has reached 96.95 %, which is close to that of the developed countries.[3]

---

[1] The State Administration of Radio Film and Television, http://www.sarft.gov.cn/

[2] CSM Media Research is a joint venture between CTR Market Research and the Kantar Media. Dedicated to TV & radio audience measurement research, CSM Media Research offers reliable and uninterrupted rating information for Hong Kong SAR and China. Data is from CSM's Report in 2008.

[3] China's State Administration of Radio, Film and Television's Report in 2009.

So is the demand for homebred TV series in international market, especially in the Southeast Asia. The Chinese culture which has a profound influence on the Asian countries has laid a solid foundation for the export of Chinese TV series in these countries. In addition, the increase in the market demand is also evidenced by the increase in the new release of TV series, the broadcast time and the transaction value.

### *10.1.2 The Need for High Quality TV Series*

There are paradoxical situations in China's TV series market. On one hand, the TV series production is large than the demand from the TV stations. On the other hand, what were broadcast on TV can barely meet quality requirements of TV stations. It's typically hard to produce high quality TV series, usually, due to the lack of experience, short shooting period, and shortage of funds. That's also why the price remained high for the high quality TV series that were produced by large TV series maker such as Huace.

Meanwhile, TV series account for 44 % of the entire TV programs broadcasted. TV series contribute to the advertisement revenue, audience rating, and the channel branding in a significant way. That's why TV stations spent more and more money on finding and buying better quality TV series.

### *10.1.3 New Media Boosts and Enlarges the Market*

Modern communication technologies, such as the internet and mobile internet, have brought fundamental change to the traditional media. Digitization and the internet have been broadly adopted in various areas such as VOD (View on Demand), which is warmly welcomed by the Netizens (Citizen of Network).[4] The percentage of internet users was 22.6 % in 2008, and reached 26 % in 2009 which is above the average level of the world. The number of Netizens in China was 0.298 billion, which is the largest in the world.[5] Such a large group of cyber citizens can well fuel the VOD platform, and the booming of the VOD, IPTV, phone TV and mobile TV combined have driven the soaring demand of the TV stations for TV series. The question is, with such growing demand for TV series, who are the suppliers of the TV series? In particular, in such a regulated industry, who are the lucky guys that could get the permit to play?

---

[4] It is defined as an entity or person actively involved in online communities and a user of the Internet, especially an avid one.

[5] China's Internet Penetration Survey 2008 and 2009, issued by China Internet Network Information Center (CNNIC).

### *10.1.4 A Government-Licensed Industry*

In the recent years, more capital for TV series has been progressively coming from the private sectors, Hong Kong, Macao, Taiwan and foreign countries, instead of only government funding. More and more non-TV stations are also engaged in TV series production, and the government's control over the TV series has been weakened. However, it doesn't mean that the TV series market already became perfectly competitive. In fact, there is still strict government supervision on TV series production as indicated by the licensing system.

The TV series production license system started from June 1st, 1986. Under this system, only the companies that got the permit license can produce TV series. There are two types of license: Class A and Class B. The former is a permanent license, and the latter is a temporary one. So getting a Class B license is the minimum requirement for any TV production. However, one Class B license can be only used for one TV series production, and it will expire automatically when the play is finished, and a new Class B license has to be applied for a new TV series. Those TV series makers who have produced at least six TV series or at least three TV soap operas (as least more than three episodes for each season) are qualified to apply for the Class A license to the SARFT. A Class A license is permanent but has to be reviewed every other year.

In addition, there is TV series censorship. Only after receiving the license and the approval of the censor can the TV series be broadcasted. In the broadcasting stage, which is after the receipts of the license, the TV series are censored by and sold to the TV stations before the broadcast. This is how censorship in China works.

### *10.1.5 Private vs. State-Owned TV Producers*

There are two types of TV series makers engaged in the TV series production: the state owned TV series maker and private ones. Compared with the state owned, the private TV series makers are relatively young due to the late opening up of the TV series market to the private companies. Yet it demonstrates a strong momentum of development thanks to its capability of quick adaptation to the market requirements, and the encouragement and support of the government policies. As a result, some quite competitive TV series makers have been born, such as the Huayi Brothers Media Group, Hairun Movies & TV Production Co., Ltd. and Zhejiang Huace Film and TV Co., Ltd., just to name a few.

Currently, more than 60 % of capital for TV series production comes from non-government sources, and the private makers have captured more than 80 % of the TV series market. There are big differences, however, among all these TV series makers in terms of their competiveness. Some large and strong companies have experience to produce over hundreds of TV series a year, in contrast, some other firms can only produce one TV series (about 20 episodes) within one or two years. Due to the severe competition, not all the TV series produced can be broadcast, and some broadcasted TV series are only shown during the non-prime time. In either way, it may cause financial loss to the company as the result of the poor sales.

## 10.2 Huace's Road to Industry Leadership

Zhejiang Huace Film and TV Co., Ltd. was founded on October 25, 2005. Mr. Meicheng Fu and Ms. Yifang Zhao are the founders of the firm. Ever since its establishment, the company focused on the production and issue of TV series and some peripheral business. Huace is a leader in the Zhejiang TV series market and among the top TV series maker in entire China. Currently, the company can produce about 300 episodes TV series every year, and the production has been increasing along with the development of the company.[6]

There are many TV series makers in the market in China now, and the market concentration rate is pretty low. However, the market share of Huace is relatively high. Among more than 414 seasons (13,294 episodes) of TV series produced with the permit of the license, six seasons of TV series (249 episodes) were made by Huace. Huace is now the second largest independent TV series maker in terms of the number of independently produced plays, and the largest maker if also including jointly produced plays with other firms.

The revenue of Huace TV series accounted for 2 % of the total market transaction value in 2008. Huace also has advantage in importing foreign TV series through its long term cooperation with TVB in Hong Kong and other overseas producers, and imported more than nine seasons (189 episodes) TV series during the same period. Its import of TV series accounted for 4 % of the total import of the domestic market, and its TV series export made up of 5.1 % of the national total TV series export.

Huace had more than 120 employees by 2011, which was doubled on a year-over-year basis, and branch offices were established in Beijing, Shenzhen, Shanghai and Taiwan, one after another, in order to integrate the cross region resources and business expansion.

## 10.3 The Core Business: TV Series Production

The main products of Huace are TV series including TV series broadcasted by TV stations, audio and visual products, and its derivative products such as advertisements. After the completion of the TV series production and receiving of the

[6] All data of Huace are from Prospectus of Huace unless indicated otherwise.

license, the TV series become vendible, and the vendibility can be sold to the TV stations by TV series maker for revenue by issuing the TV series. At the same time, the TV series maker can also sell the copyright of the audiovisual products to the audio-visual company for royalty, and receive broadcast rights revenue through VOD, IPTV, mobile phone TV and mobile TV. Its derivative products include the advertisements paid by sponsorships, implantable advertisements, TV books and some other products. TV series is Huace's core business. The total TV series sales revenue reached about 380 million RMB in 2011 with gross profit margin 60.72 %, increased by 36 % over 2010.

### *10.3.1 Supplementary Businesses: Movie Production*

Movie is another business line of Huace. Its products include the movies shown in the movie theater, the audiovisual products, and its derivative products such as advertisements. After the completion of the movie production and receiving of the license, the movies become vendible and the vendibility can be sold to the domestic theaters and share box office sales revenue. The rights of showing the movies can also be sold to the TV stations for broadcast. The copyrights can be sold to the overseas movies issuers, and the copyrights of audiovisual products can be sold to the publishers.

## 10.4 A Unique Business Model

For better understanding the uniqueness of Huace's business model, let's first take a closer look at how TV series are produced and sold. TV series are produced by a teleplay group which is a special organization form in the TV and film industry. It's a temporarily formed group for a TV series or movie production, in charged by producer and consists of various professionals. Producer is responsible for the entire TV series or movie production, production manager takes charge of the daily operation, and director oversees the shooting and the artistry.

In general, there are three ways of producing TV series. The first one is exclusive shooting: when the market potential looks promising, the risk seems relatively less, and funding is sufficient, companies usually choose the method of exclusive shooting, which means that the companies will fund the whole production process itself. In this case, the company is both the investor and the producer, so it won't be restricted by any other investors in the TV series production.

The second one is joint shooting. If the company assessed there are relatively higher risk, they will typically choose the method of joint shooting in order to reduce fund pressure and reduce the investment risk. Under this joint model, there are executive producer and non-executive producer in terms of the roles and responsibilities they assumed. The executive producer typically takes charge of the operation of the production process, fund management, and selection of cast members, while the non-executive producer will not be involved in these activities.

The third one is outsourcing shooting. The firm can purchase the copyrights from other TV series companies whose TV series were already completed and/or will be produced. This method works in this way: buying the copyrights of TV series from other domestic or foreign companies and resell the broadcast rights to the TV stations. There are two types of outsourcing shooting: buying out issuance and fiduciary issuance. The buying out issuance means that the company buys out the right of issuance exclusively for a specific period of time and a specific region, and it will assume sole responsibility for its own profits or losses. Meanwhile, the seller of the copyright and other third party entities will no longer have the right of issuance for this product for the time and the region specified. The fiduciary issuance means that the seller of the copyright confers the right to the buyer, allowing buyer to issue the TV series. Under this model, both parties negotiate the transfer price and the profit sharing percentages. Currently, the buying out issuance is what prevails in China.

### *10.4.1 The TV Production and Selling Process*

What comes after the completion of TV movies is issuance and sales. The sales of TV movies consist of pre-sales and sales. The TV series maker can market and pre-sell the TV series which is still in the shooting process. This pre-selling method is very beneficial for the TV series business as it can increase the turnover of capital and ease the financial pressure.

The pre-selling price is mainly determined by the amount of the investment, the popularity of the cast members, and the quality of the play when the TV series was not completed yet. The brand recognition and the company's creditability play a significant role in the pre-selling process. Thanks to the good quality of the TV series, high audience rating, and the mutually beneficial cooperative relationship with the TV stations, Huace can pretty much always do well in the pre-selling, and many TV stations offered to book Huace's TV series in advance. In most cases, the revenue from pre-selling can make up 50 % of the total revenue plan for Huace's TV series.

There comes the final sales stage after the completion of the TV movie and the acquirement of the license. The producer will negotiate with the TV stations for the price of their products according to the quality, production cost, and demand of the TV stations. Due to its strong sales capability, Huace can usually get a high end price.

In addition, the "terrestrial to satellite" model is commonly used. In other words, the first round of play are typically broadcast through the Terrestrial television channels and then through satellite transmission 6 month later. As is proven by experience, this model would maximize the company's sales revenue.

## 10.4.2 The Secret of Huace's Fast Growth

There are a few of "secrets" that actually drove Huace's fast growth. The secret one should be good scripts. Traditionally, the focus of the TV series production in China was on the director and the producer. However, a good script is the foundation for an excellent TV series. The quality of the script determined the quality of TV series. Huace was among the earliest companies that realized this point.

During the planning, producing and releasing process, Huace's priority was the quality of the script and whether it meets the need and requirement of the market. In particular, in the pre-selling process, the sale result is, usually, directly determined by the quality of the script. There are about 14,000 episodes TV series produced every year in China, and consequently, there should be at least 14,000 scripts. Scripts are typically finished before the shooting process when the directors select the cast members, shooting groups and funding sources. It can be imagined that, without scripts, it would be just a job of making bricks without straw for the director.

The second secret is good scriptwriters. Good quality TV series have been growing in popularity in China. Huace has positioned itself in a right market with an annual production of about 300 episodes on average, and even more than 400 episodes in 2012. Any high quality of script was written by an excellent scriptwriter. And generally speaking, it takes about 5–10 years for a scriptwriter to mature. An excellent scriptwriter is someone who has deeper understanding of the society and the taste of the general public, and a good master of the plot and character setting. Good scriptwriters are so scarce. Thanks to the distributing-stocks-to-scriptwriters model, long-term contract and exclusive arrangement, Huace has attracted plenty of outstanding scriptwriters. Therefore, the company is strong at the creativity of high quality script and can produce many good episodes and increase its market share.

The third secret is good cooperation with scriptwriters. Huace took the lead in treating the script as the core of its business. But buying the scripts is to purchase the products of the scriptwriters. Therefore, establishing a mutual beneficial relationship with scriptwriter becomes the key to success. In this regard, Huace established a very effective model in working with these distinguished scriptwriters. To be more specific: (a) Huace first selects the fine scripts for the TV series production. Unlike the typical way of the industry in China which focuses more on directors and producers, Huace treats the outstanding scriptwriters as the core of creativity of the firm, distributes stocks to the scriptwriters, and makes long term contract with them in order to secure the source of good scripts. (b) Following the US experience, Huace appoints scriptwriters as the supervisor, participating in the entire production process and advising the whole team on the artistry of the TV series.

In addition to contracting with the scriptwriters, Huace also established the script database so that the company can just pick up good scripts from the database according to the changes in the market. In general, there are two ways that company can get the scripts: buying the copyrights of the finished scripts, and commissioning a scriptwriter to write one for the company. The second approach takes two forms. One is that the company can buy the right of adoption from fictions or caricatures, then, entrust the scriptwriters to create a script. Another one is to allow the company to select the theme, then, commission the scriptwriter to write up a script in line with the theme.

Thanks to the creativity of this model, Huace, a private company founded in 2005, has already released 6 seasons TV series (249 episodes) and ranked the second among all the private producers in terms of the number of episodes and seasons of TV series.

The fourth Secret is the successful financing. In the general meeting of stockholders on July 8, 2009, the company introduced two strategic investors: ZheShang Venture Capital and Shanghai Liuhe Capital. The two investors not only injected new capital which played a significant role in improving the capital structure, supplementing working capital and expanding productivity, but also bettered the company management and its operation.

What attracted the VCs and PEs includes the following factors: (a) the policy support from the Chinese government on the cultural industry; (b) the business model of Huace which set the scripts as the core of its business; (c) the characteristics of the founder and the professionalism of the management team; and (d) brand development and TV series releasing capability.

ZheShang Venture Capital subscribed 4,242 million shares of Huace, about 10.01 % of the total shares on July 8, 2009, at a price of RMB 8.03 per share with total value of 34.04 million. In addition, the Shanghai Liuhe Capital invested 17 million Yuan, accounting for 5 % of the total shares. The price was negotiated by the two parties at a PE ratio of 9 according to the business performance of the company in 2008.

Huace got its IPO on August 12th, 2010, raising 14.12 million shares of stocks at a price of 68 Yuan per share, with PE ratio of 85.43 and the total value of 90.72 million. After the IPO, the company's total number of shares of common stock is 564.8 million. The opening price was RMB 101, and closed at RMB 107 on August 26th, 2010.

Since the creativity plays a critical role for a culture and TV company, Huace developed many ways to motivate the key employees of the company with the funds raised. The first stock compensation plan was carried out in 2011 with 6,859,500 stock options granted to 56 employees with an exercise price of 24.87 Yuan. The maturity of the option is 48 month. The options can be exercised, after 12 month since the date of the grant, in three times in the following 36 months and the proportion of each exercise is 30, 30, 40 %, respectively. The cost of the first authorization of stock option was about RMB 58.88 million and 7.13 Yuan for each option embedded value.

## 10.5 Lessons from Huace's Success

As a leading firm in the culture and television industry, Huace demonstrated a strong momentum of growth. The right positioning and focus on the quality of TV series and TV movies have not only brought profits to the company, but also enhanced its brand name in the market place. The management team and the creation team have gained rich experience in the past decade and built up some extraordinary creativity and marketing capacity. The accumulation of creation resources, production resources and issuance channels through the past effort has laid the foundation for the virtuous cycle of the firm's continued development. The success of Huace has several instrumental implications.

**Right positioning** could be one that helps Huace to achieve what they achieved. While the TV series market in China has matured gradually, there is still strong demand for the good quality TV series. The right positioning and intensive cultivation of Huace contributed to its good quality TV series production. Since its inception, Huace has produced many good quality TV series with its first tier creative talents and founding management team, explored the true essence of the traditional Chinese culture, persisted in the integration of art and business, and achieved excellence in many aspects of the TV series production such as costume, setting, stage property, film editing, sound effect, and packaging.

The price of the good quality TV series and the TV movies are also higher than the industry average. The selling price of the completed plays is about RMB 85,000 per episode, which is much higher than the industrial average of RMB 35,000 per episode and the price of the prime time, about RMB 70,000-80,000 per episode. Huace's gross profit is about 47 % and it is much higher than the industry average of about 30 %.

Due to the large number of producers and the consequently low market concentration, even these well-known producers only occupied less than 10 % of the market shares. Ever since its foundation, however, Huace has committed to the production and issuing of high quality TV series that leads to Huace's fast development and top ranking among the Chinese private producers, thanks to its right positioning at the high quality play market in the first place.

**Well-established marketing channel** is another one attributable to Huace's success. Selling and issuing is a final step to realize a company's return from its investment. Through years, Huace has established a widely spread marketing network and business cooperation with China's Central Television and more than 60 provincial and municipal TV stations, covering the mainland, Hong Kong, Macao and Taiwan. In addition, Huace also signed a strategic cooperation agreement with Golden Eagle Broadcasting System, Anhui Satellite TV, Zhejiang TV and Broadcasting Administration that are the top buyers of TV series in China, and formed a long-term cooperation with these groups in the ways such as exclusive buying out and advanced booking.

So far, through the TV stations, Audio-visual companies and new media, Huaca's issuance has covered all provinces in mainland, Hong Kong, Macao, Taiwan, and more than 30 foreign countries and regions.

The next one is Huace's **Integration of Industry Resources.** In the culture industry, the talent resources are very much scattered and the types of companies are widely varied. Huace, however, sensitively grasped the window opportunity to integrate the various resources to form long term cooperation relationships with its various partners, and laid down a solid foundation for the fast development of its business. The integration helped Huace succeed in producing high quality TV series, gain popularity among its audience, and enhance the brand of Huace. With the integration, many production managers, directors, screenwriters, and cast members became partners of Huace through various forms of collaboration, such as stock, options and strategic cooperation agreements.

### *10.5.1 Complementary Team Structure*

Finally, TV series production involves many areas and requests different talents to work together. A complementary team structure would best serve for a TV series production company, and Huace, luckily, did have such a complementary structure for its leadership team. Yifang Zhao, the General Manager of Huace, has been working in the TV industry for more than 30 years and has earned her reputation in the market. She is the founder of Huace and also the leader of the production, issuance, and core technology team. Thanks to her background and experience, she successfully led the company in team build-up and market development.

Haiyan Yu, Deputy General Manager of Huace and the general manager of the issuance department, was an anchorwoman and hostess, and now is in charge of Huace's global issuance business. She has been working for the issuance business for more than 10 years, and sold more than thousands of episodes of TV series, creating total sales revenue for Huace of more than RMB 500 million in over 30 domestic provinces and 30 foreign countries and regions.

### *10.5.2 Looking Forward*

With 910 million RMB that were raised from IPO, where will Huace go from the current point it stands?

Integration and diversification seems the direction it will move forward. By investing in Shanghai Lyceem, an online E-commerce firm, Huace intended to enter the movie and TV derivative product market. At the same time, Huace also started to test water in movie production by participating in several movies' making, such as The Empire of Fish Beauty, An Romantic Story, and A Wind Listener, and formed equity joint venture with Zhejiang Times Movie Theaters to develop movie theaters in the second and third tier cities in China. In 2011, Huace received 1.42 million RMB from its movie box office sales, and 1.05 million through its investment in movie theaters. In addition, Huace joined the hands with Haining municipal government in Zhejiang Province to build up an Action Movie and TV Series Production Base with 1959 acres of land, and launched an Experimental Zone for International Movie and TV products Collaboration.

As a privately held firm, Huace's business model is instrumental for the sustainable growth of the television industry in China. The features of the TV industry resulted in the excess demand in the domestic market over the relatively limited supply of the TV series produced by individual companies. The bottleneck of the TV series development has always been the quality of plays. Huace accurately identified this weakest link of the industry and focused its effort on high quality of script and scriptwriters, and provided a right solution to the sustainable development of this fast growing industry.

# Chapter 11
# The Window to China's New Economy—What Can We Learn from these Case Studies?

**Abstract** This ending chapter summarizes the key takeaways of the nine case studies discussed throughout the book, all of which are listed SMEs from nine different industries. From the collective, we are able to draw some conclusions that may help the readers better understand the Chinese economy from a more micro perspective, and provide the readers with some insights about Chinese industries and companies that can't be obtained by only taking a macro view and merely looking at the aggregate variables in China's economy.

**Keywords** Fiscal stimulus · Monetary policy · Upgraded industrial structure · Micro view · Vertical integration · Innovative business models

It was about 4 years ago. In an attempt to turn around the increasingly obvious downward trend of China's economic growth, which was caused by the global financial crisis, the Chinese government announced a 4-trillion RMB fiscal stimulus package in October 2008. Through the nationwide commercial banking system, massive state funds were rapidly pumped into China's economy. Among the areas that were covered by this stimulus plan was infrastructures, which include railroads, highways, and airports, and were widely considered the top beneficiaries of the stimulus. Even though there were many debates regarding the actual allocation of the stimulus funds (the majority of which were reported to have flown into large, state-owned companies) and its possible negative impact on exacerbating China's real estate bubble, its positive effect on China's GDP growth was undeniable. From 2009 to 2011, China's economy restored its high growth track, and achieved an annual GDP growth rate of 9.2, 10.4 and 9.2 %, respectively.[1]

In a similar effort to prevent the US economy from a deep dive or "double dip", the US Federal Reserve had launched its quantitative easing of monetary stimulus four times since the outbreak of the financial crisis in 2007. In late November of 2008, the first round of quantitative easing saw the Fed buying $600 billion in

[1] State Bureau of Statistics of P.R. China: http://www.stats.gov.cn, World Bank GDP Ranking Report: http://data.worldbank.org.cn/data-catalog

J. G. Wang and J. Yang, *Who Gets Funds from China's Capital Market?*, SpringerBriefs in Business, DOI: 10.1007/978-3-642-44913-0_11, 

mortgage-backed securities (MBS), and by March 2009, Fed held $1.75 trillion in bank debt, MBS, and Treasury notes, and reached a peak of $2.1 trillion in June 2010. In November 2010, the Federal Reserve announced a second round of quantitative easing, known as "QE2", buying $600 billion of Treasury securities by the end of the second quarter of 2011. A third round of quantitative easing, "QE3", was announced in September of 2012. This third round of easing included a plan to purchase USD $40 billion of mortgage-backed securities (MBS) each month until the Fed considers the US economy to be "fully recovered" from the crisis. On December 12, 2012, only 3 months after QE3 launching, Federal Reserve announced "QE4" to have more quantitative easing at a rate of $85 billion a month for an extended period until unemployment rate falls below 6.5 %, and inflation projections remain no more than half a percentage point above 2 % 2 years out.[2] However, while this massive injection of liquidity did successfully help maintain an extremely low interest rate in the US, its stimulus impact on the real sector and US GDP growth seemed unclear. The numbers tell an ambivalent story—from 2009 to 2011, US annual GDP grew by—3.5, 3 and 1.7, respectively.[3]

These seemingly different results of government stimulus policies on GDP growth in the US versus China may be considered a real life example of the potential differences in the effectiveness between monetary policy and fiscal policy. Without a question, every single fiscal dollar spent undoubtedly creates one solid dollar demand for goods and services. In contrast, the impact of generating purchase through money pumped in by monetary policy is uncertain, given that so many intermediate steps come between the start and the completion of the monetary transmission mechanism. If any of these intermediate steps don't go as planned, these funds may flow to an area that was not intended by policy makers.

However, even though the Chinese economy fundamentally appeared to benefit more from the stimulus, the capital market performance of the US and China in that same time period revealed just the opposite picture. As of early December 2012, the S&P 500 Index once jumped to 1420, getting much closer to its peak level of 1565 on October 2007, and almost doubled the level it had seen at the trough in February 2009.[4] At the same time, however, China's Shanghai Stock Exchange Composite Index, which at one point hit the 3400 in July 2009 from the trough of 1800 in November 2008, went all the way down again since then to about 2060 in early December 2012. Comparing to the trough in November 2008, it only gained by about 11 %. Compared with its peak level at October 2007, which was at about 5000, it lost almost 60 % of its market value. This loss was about 10 times bigger than the loss in the US capital market over the same period

---

[2] http://en.wikipedia.org/wiki/Quantitative_easing

[3] Federal Reserve Bank of Philadelphia: http://www.philadelphiafed.org

[4] http://www.standardandpoors.com/

of time. The only exception is China's SME Board. The SME Index has gained 183.6 % since 2005 when the board was set up, and 67.68 % since 2007. Even during financial crisis time, it still grew over 30 % annually.[5]

These seemingly contradictory statistics inevitably trigger many questions from various China market participants and observers. Among them, are China's capital markets undervalued? Are China's capital markets in line with economic fundamentals? And, more specifically, how do the performance of China's capital markets actually correlate with the performance of the Chinese economy?

While it is still unclear as to whether or not the stock market in China is the best lens through which to analyze the soundness of the Chinese economy, as there is an apparent mismatch between capital market performance and fundamental economic performance, it is definitely clear that China's capital market is a valuable window by which one can see and understand certain important aspects of the Chinese economy which can't be seen otherwise. In particular, the study of the Chinese companies such as these SMEs, especially those listed in the Chinese capital market, can help instrumentally understand the China's development at micro level, the upgrade of its industrial structure, and why certain business models adopted by leading firms in China have been so successful in such a competitive marketplace. As China's economic success is indeed built upon the success of its millions of companies, understanding the business models that these successful companies developed and adopted become critical in understanding the success of the overall Chinese economy. The nuances of these forces, which act under the surface of China's seemingly perpetual growth rates and high GDP level, are difficult to be captured by simply looking at the macro side of Chinese economy and those aggregate numbers.

The most notable takeaway from the representative cases presented in this book are these "new faces" emerged in China's upgraded industrial structure, as reflected by (but certainly are not limited to) the companies selected. As a strong sample, the nine firms chosen to be analyzed cover a wide spectrum of industries, ranging from modern agriculture, alternative energy, and natural resource recycling to mobile internet, supply chain logistics, and financing, luxury products, and entertainment. In contrast to the stereotypical perception of the traditional Chinese economy—products marked "made in China" and linked to some low-end, "low-tech" industries such as dollar store products or cheap Wal-Mart apparel—the companies and industries represented in this book are very much ones of the twenty-first century.

The second important learning from the cases studied in this book is the understanding of the perspective and needs of China's domestic market. While all the companies cased in this book have the potential to export their products or services overseas—especially the hybrid car manufacturer—most of these firms' primary markets, such as agriculture, recycling, mobile-internet have a firm

[5] Stock Index in China: http://www.indexfunds.com.cn, Shanghai Stock Exchange: http://www.sse.com.cn/market/sseindex/, Shenzhen Stock Exchange: http://www.szse.cn/main/marketdata/

domestic focus. This domestic focus is likely to continue in at least the foreseeable future. Therefore, these companies' listing in the China's capital market and their receiving of the equity funds from various investors revealed a very important message, that is, the perspective of China's domestic market is not only favored by policy makers, scholars, or even industry analysts by their articles and speeches, but also endorsed by the investors by their real actions of fund investment. It is important to notice that it is the investors that finally determine the realization of any "potentials" in any markets.

Third, these case studies disclose telling trends in the development strategies of the successful, modern Chinese SMEs. No matter if it's Western Husbandry in agriculture, Palm Game in mobile internet, or Hua Yi Brothers in entertainment, many of these companies are trending towards the vertical integration of their respective supply chains. As the concept of supply chain advantage evolves, supply chain management in China is fundamentally changing the way these companies compete in the market place. Competition is no longer limited to one company against another; it became the competition of one supply chain competing against another supply chain. The increasing co-dependency between companies on all levels of a single supply chain has demonstrated that only by harnessing efficiency throughout the entire chain, can any of these companies succeed.

The fourth part that should be highlighted from the text is the transition of China's economy from a low end "made in China" model to a model focused higher up on the supply chain—the "designed in China" model, one reflected by the cases presented in this book. Alpha Animation is a representative case in point. In the toy industry, China is, no doubt, the workshop of the world. More than 70 % of the toys sold in the global market every year are manufactured in China. However, as manufacturing only represents the lowest spot in value chain, the profitability of Chinese toy makers is often extremely low. The Chinese factory price is only about 1 % of the eventual retail price in the US. Therefore, ascending from the low end of the value chain was the only way for Chinese toy makers to survive in the post-financial crisis era when global demands became sluggish. As the leading firm in this effort, Alpha Animation was among the first group of the Chinese companies that not only manufactured the toys, but also designed its own animated figures. From 2006 to 2009, in a 3-year time span, Alpha Animation obtained over 100 patents each year on average, and developed a sequence of animated figures, including Auldey, that proved extremely popular with Chinese consumers. In addition to manufacturing their own custom-designed animated figures, Alpha Animation also made animated movies to complement these custom figures. This double channel strategy, backed by the solid success of their animated creations, caused Alpha Animation to rise to the top as a "design" leader in what had previously only been a "made in China" industry. It gained a unique position as a leading Chinese toymaker in a market dominated by famous international brands such as Toys' R Us of the US and Bandai of Japan.

Finally, the creativity and uniqueness of some of the business models discussed in the cases highlight the remarkable (and ever-rising) level of innovation that is now present in Chinese industries, a topic that merits a deeper dive. We can first take a look at the case of Xinjiang Western Animal Husbandry Co. As a company in the dairy industry in China, quality and safety control is a salient issue that the company has had to battle with in the past decade following the incident of San Lu Milk. The powdered milk crisis, which not only shocked the entire nation, had also almost destroyed the reputation of the entire dairy industry in China. The reality is, however, that controlling the quality and safety of dairy products in China is actually an incredibly complicated task for many of these large dairy companies, given such scattered suppliers, especially at the upper end. As evidenced by countries such as the US, a very effective way to control the quality and safety of milk while simultaneously gaining economy of scale is to centralize the supply of milk sources. Many countries do this by obtaining milk from fewer but larger-sized husbandry farms. In China, however, the percentage of farms with 30 or more cows was only about 30 %; quantity-wise, the smaller-sized Chinese cow farms only produced about 1 % of the country's milk supply. Most of this was due to the shortage of large areas of suitable land or climate, lack of funds, and lack of well-trained agriculture technicians. This hard reality made it difficult, if not impossible, for Western Animal Husbandry to achieve widespread the level of quality and safety control as well as economy of scale through US-like models of centralization.

Facing this environment, Western Husbandry creatively developed a "parallel development strategy," a kind of "second best" strategy to control milk quality. On one hand, it began to steadily build up larger farms to resolve the issue of quality control from a fundamental level, which also allowed the company to capture much high level of economies of scale from production. Their plan targeted to build up a farm with up to 6000 cows, and was made possible through an IPO and public financing. Simultaneously, Western Husbandry "centralized" and standardized a service package to the hundreds of smaller farmers outside of the company's direct control, a package which used the same standards as those applied to Western Husbandry's own large farm. This package covered the areas of seeding, feed, grass cutting, milking, transportation and other stages of the supply chain. Following this "decentralized centralization and standardization" model, the whole process of producing milk, with the only exception of the "decentralized" location of the suppliers, was pretty much under the control of Western Husbandry. Meanwhile, the company was able to enjoy the economy of scale from the operation.

Another example of the creativity of the business model is the "cross-industry" integration strategy of BYD, a new-energy-driven-car manufacturer. Recognized as a leading car-maker due to their use of alternative energy, BYD was favored by many worldwide investors, including Warren Buffet. But its leading position in the new-energy-powered car industry was actually, and primarily, a result of its activities outside of the car manufacturing industry. As a new-energy-driven car using electric and other non-traditional energy, the battery used by a car is the most critical element to success. As a leading company in re-chargeable battery industry, BYD had over 100 patents in Lithium iron phosphate battery techniques which possess better safety features, longer recycle time, less pollution, and lower production costs compared to the batteries of its competitors. It took advantage of these lucrative patents, along with other innovations such as the double-mode power system, to enter the car industry as an alternative-energy car manufacturer. Even though BYD is not a yet a top leading firm in the car industry as a whole, which includes cars powered by traditional gas, it quickly took the leading position in the sub-industry field of alternative-energy vehicles. The synergy and "energy" generated by this cross-industry integration makes BYD a critical competitor to watch for in both battery and car industries.

Supply chain financing developed by Eternal Asia is another interesting model that may have a large impact on small business financing as a whole. As a supply chain management firm, Eternal Asia was one of the first to successfully develop a fully-functional one-stop-shopping supply chain service for its various customers. Eternal Asia's supply chain services cover not only traditional purchasing and distribution, but also transportation, warehouse management, customs, special tax zone, clearance, maintenance, and payment services. In other words, it covers almost everything that a company may encounter along its supply chain. But what actually distinguished Eternal Asia from its competitors is the financing service it provided to its customers. As many customers of Eternal Asia are medium and small sized firms that typically had difficulties obtaining financing from banks in China, Eternal Asia took advantage of its status as a large firm with sound creditability to borrow from banks themselves, then subsequently lending these borrowed funds to their smaller clients who required financing. Because it was the core company in the supply chain, Eternal Asia knew and understood much more about the operations and financials of the borrowing firms than banks, since these firms are also Eternal Asia's supply chain clients. As a result, this financing model significantly reduced the uncertainty and risk associated with asymmetric information issues, hence reducing the cost of financing for the small businesses and accelerating international trade flows. As discussed in the case, the issue of small business financing represents a huge challenge worldwide, and supply chain financing could be instructive in developing solutions to this challenge.

In a highly customized market such as the yacht industry, simply gaining profitability through economy of scale could be a puzzling issue. But the business model developed by Sun Bird rose to this challenge in a creative and intriguing way. As is well known by connoisseurs, the yacht industry is marked by highly diversified and highly customized demands from its end customers. Typically, the majority of the yacht makers use a customization approach to making yachts, a production model that makes reducing cost through economy of scale particularly difficult. However, Sun Bird successfully resolved this issue by creating a "standardization + customization" model. Using this model, Sun Bird prepared more than 1000 different yacht designs for customers to select from, effectively satisfying almost every one of the diversified, customized client demands. Meanwhile, because these 1000 blueprints were Sun Bird's own creations, they were able to standardize and modulate the parts that went into them, no matter how different the final yacht design. As a result, they were able to capture economies of scale from production, while simultaneously catering to their customers' diverse desires. This model quickly brought the Sun Bird to the leading position in China's yacht industry.

Finally, entertainment is another industry that has rapidly developed in China in the past decade. When the Chinese government lifted its entry barrier for privately-owned entertainment companies, a few movie makers immediately rose to the top, securing a significant share of today's rapidly expanding entertainment market in China. Among them, Huayi Brothers is no doubt one of the shining stars. Since its inception in 1994, Huayi adopted a very unique business model from which they managed to grow rapidly. Among its success recipe, the first element is to target celebrities as the main private equity investors in addition to other "regular" investors. They successfully convinced some big names such as Ma Yun, the owner and CEO of Alibaba to invest in Huayi Brothers, and the "celebrity effect" brought more investors and more funds to the company. As a consequence, Huayi always had an advantage over its competitors when it came to available funds. Second, in addition to being a movie maker, Huayi also played the role of agent for many entertainers. They wrote scripts that fit the style of the directors and actors/actresses they signed on, and meanwhile used the reputation of these directors and actors/actresses to enhance the ticket sales of their movies. In addition, in order to secure strong, long-term relationships with these movie directors, play-writers and star actors/actresses, Huayi awarded them company's stock and made them company's shareholders. Finally, Huayi developed its own movie theaters in order to integrate the entire supply chain to make it under their control. So far, it has built five movie theaters in five different cities in China, and this vertical integration has significantly enhanced the continued profitability of the Huayi Brothers.

## 11.1 Final Words

November of 2012 was a month that attracted the attention of the world. As President Obama won his second term for White House in the United States, huge decisions regarding China's new leadership for the next decade were also being made, decisions that would affect where China will go in the next 10 years, and whether China will be able to continue its decades-long economic growth. These factors were undoubtedly the focal point for policy makers, business leaders, equity and debt investors, academic researchers, and all individuals worldwide whose personal and financial stakes may be impacted in one way or another by what will happen in China. Even though nobody knows for sure what will happen in an increasingly uncertain world, it is more or less a sound consensus among academics and policy makers that China will continue its current growth track for the next few decades. There is also a possibility that China may surpass US as the most powerful generator of GDP growth around 2020 or later. As a result, China continues to represent the "new frontier" for the business community worldwide, at least in the foreseeable future. Understanding the upgrade in China's industry structure, China's emerging areas, the successful business models that help the Chinese companies succeed in a highly competitive market, or in general, understanding the micro foundation of the Chinese economy will be critical for any "stakeholders" in the Chinese economy in the coming years. We hope that this book of case studies on small and medium sized companies that were listed in China's stock market, which focuses on the micro side and company level of the Chinese economy, can provide a valuable window through which all the stakeholders and observers of the Chinese economy can enhance their knowledge and understanding about Chinese economy in the twenty-first century.

# Index




J. G. Wang and J. Yang, *Who Gets Funds from China's Capital Market?*,
SpringerBriefs in Business, DOI: 10.1007/978-3-642-44913-0, © The Author(s) 2013

MIX
Papier aus verantwortungsvollen Quellen
Paper from responsible sources
FSC® C105338

If you have any concerns about our products,
you can contact us on
**ProductSafety@springernature.com**

In case Publisher is established outside the EU,
the EU authorized representative is:
**Springer Nature Customer Service Center GmbH**
**Europaplatz 3, 69115 Heidelberg, Germany**

Printed by Libri Plureos GmbH
in Hamburg, Germany